KB204038

궁금하세요? 우리 절집

HANDBOOK FOR EXPLORING KOREAN TEMPLES

(English & Korean Edition)

영한 대역 한국 사찰 가이드

궁금하세요? 우리 절집

HANDBOOK FOR EXPLORING KOREAN TEMPLES

고연희 엮음

운주사

Preface

After I became a member of IDIA (International Dharma Instructors' Association) in the Jogye Order in 2000, I worked as a volunteer interpreter for foreign tourists at Jogyesa Temple. I used to explain about the Buddhas enshrined in the halls, stupa, a short history of the Jogye Order, and I answered to questions if they asked. It lasted until 2008 when I had to quit to take care of my grandson, like most Korean housewives of old age do.

Some foreign tourists who came to Jogyesa temple from Beomeosa in Busan via Tongdohsa in Yangsan or Haeinsa in Daegu were disappointed looking around the small temple compounds that is the headquarters of Korean Buddhism. Others, who came through main land China, loved praising the bright, pleasant, and lively atmosphere of the temple. At that time, I could not recognize what they said, since I took it for granted, until I had a chance to visit many temples in China some years later.

Welcoming as a co-host country for the 2002 World Cup, the Korean Buddhist Society was strained as well. This was because the Korean government decided to use some Buddhist temples to supplement the country's accommodation facilities and introduce Korean buddhist culture to abroad. A one-year period was not a long time for the preparation of selecting temples, recruiting volunteer workers who were good at English, and training them. Staff workers in the Jogye Order invited Ambassadors to Korea and their families for a simulated practice of Templestay. As a Vice President of the IDIA, I took part in preparing this event with the Order, publishing a book, *Guide to Korean Buddhist Temples*, and making a cassette tape, *the Biography of the Buddha for Children,* with our IDIA members.

Around that time I was asked by the weekly Buddhist Newspaper, Beopbo Shinmun (법보신문), to write a short article to introduce Korean Temples every week. It was the first attempt to write in English on the Buddhist Newspaper. I worked the job for 6 months. This book is based on that series of articles, and I added some more by recollecting the experiences in Jogyesa Temple. It has passed more than 10 years that I have not read or spoken English. I have forgotten most English Buddhist terminologies. Besides that, website situations have changed, far different from those of 2001 or 2002. Today, anybody can access websites to search for any information they want through Google or Naver just by several times touching their mobile screen. Thinking of this, it looks very foolish and useless of me to write such a book, as an ordinary buddhist, neither a monk nor a scholar.

The form of this book is composed of "an international visitor's question and my answer." It is not necessarily for foreigners but for Koreans who are Buddhism-friendly but

Buddhism-blinds (one who can understand English), and to cover my poor English ability to describe.

"Do no evil./ Do only good./ Cleanse the mind./ This is the teaching of all the Buddhas." These sentences, as one of the basic teachings of Buddhism, are simple and easy to understand. However, when it is written in Chinese-based Korean, it became difficult to read and understand: 諸惡莫作/ 衆善奉行/ 自淨其意/ 是諸佛敎 or 제악막작/ 중선봉행/ 자정기의/ 시제불교.

It is very good that the Three Pitakas are completely translated into Korean now. But even Korean Sutras do not make sense to me from time to time. That is why I began reading English Sutras, and it has helped me greatly. Most Korean students learn English very hard at school to enter university. I stronly suggest that young monks in the future should study English Sutras along with Sutras written in Chinese letters in the Sangha University or in *Kangwon*. Then, why not open an English Sutra class at temples? This would be killing two birds with one stone; to disseminate, and to communicate with young ones, who are potential buddhists, through English Sutras. That was the way I read the Bible at the English Bible class in my high school days. Many Buddhist parents will send their children to the temples to learn English and Buddha's Teachings.

I would like to thank Professor Scott Scattergood in Ajou University for his willingness and generous help to proofreading precisely.

I want to send my love to my daughter (Jung-im Hwang) and son (Chang-suck Hwang), who gave me joy and courage every time troubles came to me. Finally, I deeply appreciate President Si-yol Kim in Unjusa Publishing Co., who made up his mind to publish this book written in both Korean and English, even in the midst of a recession due to Covid 19.

Any mistakes and incorrect explanations in this book are, of course, solely the faults of my shabby and humble knowledge. I dedicate this book to my dead parents, who gave me a sound body and mind, and opportunities for good education in those hard times after the Korean War.

May all beings be well and happy!
With palms together,
September in 2021 (the second year of Covid 19 outbreak)

들어가는 말

2000년에 조계종단의 국제포교사 품수를 받고 나서 국제포교사회의 일과 함께 조계사 외국인 안내소에서 자원봉사를 했다. 외국인 관광객을 상대로 조계사 경내를 안내하고 한국불교에 대해 설명해 주는 일이었다. 2008년, 한국의 많은 할머니들이 겪는 황혼육아로 현장을 떠날 때까지 만 8년을 조계사에서 보낸 셈이다.

외국인 중에는 부산 범어사를 시작으로 양산 통도사, 합천 해인사를 거쳐서 조계사 경내를 돌아보고는 규모면에서 엄청 실망하는 사람이 있는가 하면, 중국의 사찰을 거쳐서 온 사람들 중에는 밝고 깨끗하고 활기찬 우리 절 분위기를 좋아하는 이들도 많았다. '절이 당연히 밝고 깨끗하지'라는 생각에 당시에는 그런 말이 의아했는데 훗날 중국 사찰을 직접 가보니 그 말의 의미를 알 수 있었다.

일본과 공동 주최국이었던 2002년 월드컵 경기를 준비하면서 우리 불교계도 긴장하고 있었다. 부족한 숙박시설을 보완하고 한국의 불교문화를 알리는 좋은 기회로 삼아 산문을 열기로 결정했기 때문이다. 그러한 목적에 알맞은 사찰을 지정하고, 자원봉사자를 모집하여 사찰 안내 훈련과 책자를 만들고, 서울 주재 외국 대사들을 초청해서 모의 템플스테이 실습도 해 보고, 일 년이 짧았다.

한편 국제포교사회는 당시 종단과 협조하여 외국인을 위한 템플스테이를 준비하면서 한국불교를 알리는 영문 단행본(Guide to

Korean Buddhist Temples)과 어린이를 위한 부처님 일대기(the story of the Buddha for Children)를 카세트테이프로 제작하여 펴내는 일을 해냈다. 그 즈음에 법보신문에서 영문으로 절집을 안내하는 꼭지를 하나 써달라는 부탁을 받고 겁 없이 수락을 해서 6개월 동안 연재했다. 이 책은 그때의 원고를 기본으로 하고, 조계사 시절의 경험을 살려서 몇 꼭지를 더 보태고, 그밖에 다른 영문 불교지에 발표했던 원고도 끌어 모아 엉성하게 엮은 것이다. 손자를 키우면서 영어에서 손을 뗀 지 10여 년이 넘는 세월에 그나마 알고 있던 불교 용어도 가물가물했다. 코로나19로 꼼짝없이 갇혀 있으면서 영문판 불교서적을 다시 읽으며 작업을 시작했지만 읽어도 금방 잊어버리는 나이는 어쩔 수 없었다.

이 책은 외국인(F)이 물으면 그에 답하는(K) 형식을 빌렸는데, 이는 반드시 외국인을 위한 것이기보다는 한국인이면서도 불교를 너무 모르고 무슨 미신 취급하는 불교 문맹자들(그러나 영어를 이해하는 사람들)을 대상으로 했다는 것이 솔직한 마음이다. 또한 불교 전공자도 아니고 어디까지나 평범한 불자에 불과한 필자가 불교를 알리는 데는 한계가 있을 수밖에 없으니 문어체보다는 대화체가 짧은 내 영어 실력을 커버할 수도 있겠다 싶어서 택한 고육책이기도 하다.

처음 원고를 썼던 2001년도와 지금의 웹 환경이 엄청 변한 것을 모르는 바가 아니다. 네이버나 구글에 들어가면 원하는 정보를 해결해주는 시대인데 쓸데없는 짓 하고 있다는 생각이 머리를 떠나지 않았다. 그동안 모아놓은 자료들을 그냥 없애기 아까워서 벌인 일이니 넓은 아량으로 헤아려주길 부탁드릴 뿐이다.

"Do no evil, Do only good, Cleanse the mind, This is the teaching of all the Buddhas. 이 문장은 중학생 정도만 되어도 깊은 뜻까지는 아니더라도 쉽게 이해할 수 있다. 그런데 이것을 "제악막작諸惡莫作 중선봉행衆善奉行 자정기의自淨其意 시제불교是諸佛教"라 쓰면 이해할까? 이쯤 되면 불교 공부를 영어로 하면 쉽지 않을까 생각해 봄직하다.

요즈음은 우리말 팔만대장경이 있어 마음만 먹으면 얼마든지 경전을 읽을 수 있다. 정말 다행스런 일이다. 그런데 우리글로 읽어도 뜻이 들어오지 않을 때가 많다. 법회 때마다 독송하는 반야심경도 그러하니 다른 경전인들 얼마나 다르랴? 영어로 경전을 읽고, 공부하자고 마음먹은 이유이고, 이렇게 자료를 정리하는 이유이다.

승가대학이나 강원에서 한자로 된 경전만을 강독할 것이 아니라 영어 경전 강독도 필수과목으로 해야 된다고 감히 제안한다. 대한민국처럼 영어공부를 열심히 시키는 나라가 또 어디 있을까? 온 국민을 영어 콤플렉스에 빠지게 하는 나라인데, 젊은 스님들이 예비 불자들인 젊은 학생들과 소통하는 한 방법으로 영어로 경전을 읽고 부처님의 가르침을 편다면, '나 같은 나이든 불자들이 다 떠나고 나면 과연 불교 인구가 얼마나 될까' 하는 걱정은 안 해도 되지 않을까. 옛날 고교 시절에 영어성경반에서 성경 공부를 했듯이 절마다 영어 경전반을 개설하면 어떨까? 불자 가정마다 아이들을 절에 보낼 것이다. 영어도 공부하고, 부처님 법도 공부하고, 스님들은 저절로 포교가 되어 좋고, 일석 삼조가 아니겠는가? 미래에 불교가 살아

남을 수 있는 길이 과연 '절에서 하룻밤 묵으며 절 분위기 체험하는 템플스테이로 충분할까?'

꼼꼼하게 교정을 봐 주신 아주대학교 스캇 교수님께 감사드린다.

내가 힘들 때마다 버팀목이 되어준 우리 아이들(黃湞壬/昶錫)에게 고맙다는 말을 전하고 싶다. 마지막으로 코로나 19로 모두가 힘든 때에 영문까지 곁들인 원고를 받아주신 불서출판 운주사 대표 김시열 사장님께 진심으로 감사의 말을 전한다.

부족한 표현이나 잘못된 설명은 전적으로 나의 이해 부족과 잘못임을 밝히면서, 이 책을 한국전쟁 후 그 힘든 시절, 없는 살림에도 4남매를 곱게, 바르게 길러주신 돌아가신 부모님 영전에 삼가 드린다.

2021년 9월
삼보 귀의하옵고
고연희(묘심월) 합장

Part 1 **Key Information** • 17

Part 2   Outside the Compound · 79

Part 3   Inside the Compound · 97

Part 4 **Halls and Shrines** • 147

Part 1

Key Information

1. Taking Refuge in the Three Jewels (Gems)
삼보 귀의

All Buddhists' ceremonies begin with declaring and confirming the "Taking refuge in the three jewels: I take refuge in the Buddha. I take refuge in the Dharma, I take refuge in the Sangha." Buddhists' worship is to show our respect and gratitude by prostration to the Three Jewels: Buddha, historical Buddha; Dharma, his teachings; and Sanga, the Buddhist community of monks and nuns.

The historical Buddha, S(h)akyamuni was not a son of an almighty God who will save or punish us, but was born as an ordinary human being, who attained unexcelled, complete, perfect Awakening through his own cultivation. He is a great teacher who shows us the same way to the goal which he attained. He delivered that every ordinary being can attain the ultimate liberation by learning and practicing following the 'path' he found. This is because we are already endowed with Buddha-nature, the potentiality to be a buddha.

The Dharma helps us to see the true nature of existence, the ultimate reality. To do this, we should keep our mind free of the idea 'I', or 'mine'. Ordinary beings do not see things as they really are. They see things as they want or like with attachment and clinging of 'I' and 'mine', due to karmic habitual energy of previous and present lives. This causes relentless suffering.

In the Dharma, everything is a result of a complex of cause and conditions; that is the principle of dependent co-rising (연기법). Nothing exists on its own. *When this exists, that exists; on the arising of this, that arises. When this does not exist, that does not come to be; on the cessation of this, that ceases.*

The Sangha is the group of monks and nuns who renounce worldly desires, devoting themselves to practice to be liberated from delusion. Thanks to their dedication for transmitting Buddha's Teaching to next generation, the light of Law has been kept and enables us to lead a better life.

모든 불전 의식은 삼보 귀의—"부처님께 귀의합니다 / (부처님의) 가르침에 귀의합니다 / 승가에 귀의합니다"—의 염송으로 시작된다. 불교의 예배는 삼보(부처님과 가르침과 승단)께 감사와 존경을 오체투지로 표현하는 것이다.

역사적인 부처님, 석가모니 부처님은 우리를 벌주거나 구원해 줄 수 있는 무슨 전지전능한 신의 아들이 아니라, 평범한 인간으로 태어나서 스스로의 수행력으로 무상 정등 정각을 이루신 분이다. 우리도 부처님처럼 성불할 수 있는 잠재력, 불성을 갖추고 있기 때문에, 가르침대로 배우고 수행하면 성불할 수 있다는 '길'을 가르쳐주시고 보여주신 분이다.

부처님의 가르침(법)은 '나'와 '내 것'이라는 생각에서 벗어나 궁극의 실재, 존재의 본질을 제대로 볼 것을 가르친다. 중생들은 과거 생과 현생의 업력과 습기로 '나와 내 것'이라는 아집과 집착 때문에 존재의 본질을 있는 그대로 보지 못하고, 보고 싶은 대로만 보기 때문에 고통을 벗어날 수 없다고 가르친다. 모든 것은 인연의 집합이고 홀로 존재하는 것은 하나도 없다는 연기의 가르침을 강조한다. "이것이 있음으로 저것이 있고, 이것이 생함으로 저것이 생한다. 이것이 없음으로 저것이 없고, 이것이 멸함으로 저것이 멸한다."

승가는 세속의 모든 욕망을 여의고 오직 번뇌에서 해탈하겠다는 서원을 세운 비구와 비구니의 공동체를 말한다. 승가의 헌신으로 전등(傳燈; 법을 전함)의 빛이 꺼지지 않고 이어져서 우리를 일깨워주고 있기에 우리는 삼보께 귀의하는 예를 다하는 것이다.

2. Three Marks of Existence
(Three Dharma Seals)
삼법인

F: Could you kindly share me with the Three Marks of Existence (Three Dharma Seals) in Buddhism?

K: With pleasure. They are the attributes of all existences: impermanence, suffering, and no-self. As the core of Buddha's teaching, they were an unorthodox doctrine at the time of Buddha, when the notion of 'atman' prevailed. The Brahmins thought that each being possessed a pure and eternal Self (Atman) that transmitted from one life to the next.

F: I can understand the teaching that everything is impermanent, and that causes suffering. However, the concept of no-self fills me with doubt. Do I have to deny myself as a student and tourist who is talking and enjoying life? All the more, we have been educated emphasizing individuality and personality at school.

K: I understand what you mean. The 'No-self teaching' does not deny you as an individual being conditioned by a combination of mental and physical aggregates. Essentially, in terms of ultimate truth (진제), you have no fixed, unchanging, and permanent self. However, phenomenally, in terms of conventional truth (속제), you actually exist as a son, a student and so on. Where phenomena is, there is a function, and then causes and effects follow. From this teaching, the Buddha warned us not to cling to anything, especially 'I' and 'mine'. We are nothing but a complex of causes and conditions without substantiality, existing in dependent co-rising. Therefore, these three teachings are interrelated and interdependent. The no-self concept developed into the theory of the Emptiness (Void) in Mahayana Buddhism.

F: I see. If there's nothing fixed, no permanent self, what about rebirth? What is transmitted from life to life?

K: It has been a long debate, and is not precisely resolved. Often an example of 'a flame passed from one lamp to another' has been used. The following flame is functionally connected with the former and the succeeding one, but with no identity. As we know, whenever some conditions come together, there are surely some effects interdependently. Due to no eternal, permanent self, rebirth occurs just the same as this law of cause and effect. (무아윤회)

F: 삼법인에 관해서 설명해 주시겠어요?

K: 그럼요. 삼법인三法印은 부처님의 핵심 사상으로, 존재의 속성에 관한 가르침이죠. 무상無常, 고苦, 무아無我의 가르침이 그것이죠. 아트만 사상이 팽배해 있던 당시에 아주 독특한 사상이었지요.

당시 브라만들은 변하지 않는 영원하고 순수한 자아가 있어 그것이 윤회한다고 생각했지요.

F: 변하지 않는 것은 없다는 무상과 그것 때문에 고통이 있다는 가르침은 이해가 되는데요, 무아에 관해서는 좀 의아해요. 내가 분명히 학생으로서, 관광객으로 여기 존재해서 말하고 즐기고 있는 나를 부정하는 거잖아요? 더구나 우리가 학교에서는 개성과 인성을 강조하는 교육을 받았는데요.

K: 무슨 말 하는지 알아요. 무아의 가르침이 정신적 물질적 결합체로서의 나를 부정하는 것이 아닙니다. 진제眞諦적인 입장에서는 본질적으로 변하지 않는 영원한 속성의 나는 없지만, 속제俗諦로서, 즉 현상적 입장에서는 나는 아들로, 학생으로 등등으로 엄연히 존재하지요. 현상적으로 존재하니 작용이 있고 이로 인해 인과가 생기는 것이죠. 그래서 부처님께서는 어느 것에도, 특히 나와 내 것에 집착하지 말라고 경고하신 겁니다. 우리는 다만 인연따라 존재하는 연기적 존재라는 것이죠. 삼법인의 가르침은 세 가지의 가르침이 서로서로 연관되어 있는 상의적인 가르침입니다. 무아사상이 대승불교에서 공사상으로 발전하지요.

F: 알겠어요. 그런데 무아라면서 윤회는 어떻게 설명해요? 무엇이 윤회를 만들지요?

K: 그게 오래된 논쟁거리지요. 명료하게 설명되고 있지 않지만 램프로 이어지는 불꽃을 예로 들어서 설명하곤 해요. 램프에 붙여진 불꽃이 앞의 것과 같은 작용을 갖고 상속이 되고 있지만 똑같은 불꽃이 아니지요. 영속적인 불변하는 자아가 없기에 연(조건)

이 모여지면 서로에 의존하면서 그 결과는 반드시 있게 마련이 니까 윤회도 이런 식으로 일어나는 겁니다. (무아윤회)

불교의 핵심 이론인 제법무아를 처음에 공부하면서 '우리는 모두 연기 로 존재한다. 연기는 인연생기因緣生起의 줄임말이다'라고 그냥 외웠 다. 영어로 연기를 dependent origination이라 배웠지만 그 뜻이 쉽게 와 닿지 않았다. dependent arising 또는 dependent co-rising이란 번 역이 좀 더 쉽다. 모든 존재는 홀로 존재할 수 없고, 모든 존재가 연결 되어 서로가 서로에게 존재의 근거가 되어 주고 있는 것이다.
얼마 전 신문에서 '공생적 온존(Symbiotic wellbeing)'이라고 표현한 것을 보고 불자뿐 아니라 비불자들에게도 이런 표현이라면 연기가 쉽게 와 닿지 않을까 하는 생각을 했다. Covid19 사태로 전 지구가 앓고 있는 요즈음에 연기를 생각하며 인간의 탐진치를 반성해야 할 텐데, 코로나 의 연(조건)이 사라질 그때는 언제쯤일까?

Three (Four) Marks (Seals) of Existence (三/四法印)

1) Nothing is permanent. (Everything constantly changes) :
   諸行無常
2) All things are suffering. : 一切皆苦
3) Nothing has a fixed, permanent self. : 諸法無我
4) Nirvana is ultimately tranquil. : 涅槃寂靜
   (무상, 고, 무아의 삼법인에서 열반적정을 포함해 사법인을 얘기하기도
   한다.)

3. Half bowing

합장 반배

(in front of the One Pillar Gate)

K: Passing through this gate, you should show respect like this. (demonstrating bowing) We call this half bowing with palms together in front of your chest, *Hap-jang Ban-bae* in Korean.

F: I have seen you do that every time you came across monks in the street on our way to the temple.

K: Have you! Good eye! This is one of the traditional ways of bowing in Korean Buddhism. I'll show you the other, full bowing, in the Main Buddha Hall later.

F: Is there any special meaning to holding your palms together?

K: Among many explanations, it mainly represents one mind taking refuge in the Three Jewels (Triple Gem).

F: What is Three Jewels?

K: They represent the Buddha, Dharma, his Teaching, and Sangha or the Monastic Community.

(일주문 앞에서)

K: 이 문을 지날 때는 이렇게 인사를 해야 돼요. (반배를 하며) 우리

말로는 합장 반배라고 하는데, 두 손을 모으고 허리를 굽혀 인사하는 겁니다.

F: 여기 오는 길에 당신이 스님을 만날 때마다 그렇게 하는 것을 봤어요.

K: 그랬어요? 잘 보았네요. 우리 절집에서 하는 전통적인 인사법이지요. 두 가지가 있는데, 한 가지는 대웅전에 들어가서 자세히 설명해 드릴게요.

F: 합장을 하는 특별한 이유가 있나요?

K: 네, 여러 가지로 설명하기도 하는데, 삼보에 귀의하는 일심을 표현한다고 해요.

F: 삼보는 무엇인데요?

K: 그건 부처님과 부처님의 가르침과 승단을 말해요.

일반적으로 스님을 표현할 때 monk라는 단어를 쓰는데 아무개 스님이라고 할 때는 venerable을 쓴다. 그런데 국제포교사회에서 *Guide to Korean Buddhist Temples*를 펴냈을 때(2002년) 우리말의 '스님'을 그대로 영어로 표기해서 썼다. 적어도 우리나라에 왔으면 스님이라는 단어쯤은 알고 갔으면 하는 바람에서였다. 참고로 조계종(Jogye Order)에서 쓰는 공식적인 영문 표기 호칭을 보면, 주지는 Abbot, 선사는 Zen Master, 방장은 Spiritual Leader, 종정은 Supreme Patriarch, 총무원장은 Executive Director of Administration.

4. How to Prostrate / Full bowing
오체투지

(At the Main Buddha Hall)

F: Do you remember you were going to teach me how to prostrate in the Main Buddha Hall?

K: Yes, sure I do. Don't you flinch from bowing to the Buddha image?

F: No. Why do you ask?

K: Because many non-Buddhist Koreans regard bowing to the Buddha image as idol worshipping. Well, the best way to bow is to watch how Korean Buddhists do it and follow them.

F: Come on, buddy.

K: Just kidding. I will show you step-by-step, with brief explanations. To begin with, stand with your back erect, putting your palms together at your chest. Then kneel down to the floor putting your two hands down, parallel, and touch your forehead to the floor between your hands. Now, cross your feet, the left over the right. Then, turn your hands palm-up and raise them to about ear level, showing respect to the Buddha, and recite "I take refuge in the Buddha." Rise by reversing the order. On the second bow you recite, "I take refuge in the Dharma", and on third "I take refuge in the Sangha." After the last bow just before standing up, whether you did 3 or 108 or more, touch your forehead to the floor once again with palms up to ears, make a wish what you would like to come true to the Buddha and Bodhisattva.

F: 법당에 가서 오체투지 하는 법을 가르쳐준다고 한 것 기억해요?

K: 그럼, 그런데 정말로 절하는 것에 아무런 거리낌이 없어요?

F: 네, 없어요. 그런데 왜 그런 걸 물어요?

K: 어떤 사람들은 부처님께 절하는 것을 우상숭배라고 하거든요. 그건 그렇고, 한국 불자들이 어떻게 절하나 보고 따라하면 돼요.

F: 그러지 말고...

K: 농담이고요. 설명하면서 보여줄게요. 우선 똑바로 서서 합장을 한 다음 무릎을 꿇고 무릎 앞쪽에 두 손을 바닥에 평행이 되게 놓아요. 그리고 머리를 숙여서 두 손 사이에서 이마가 바닥에 닿게 절하는 겁니다. 이때 발은 오른발 위에 왼발이 교차하도록 합니다. 그리고 나서 두 손 바닥을 귀 높이까지 올려서 부처님을 받드는 자세를 취하면서 "부처님께 귀의합니다"라고 말합니다. 일어날 때는 반대 순서로 합니다. 두 번째 절을 할 때는 "가르침에 귀의합니다"라고 말하고, 세 번째는 "스님들께 귀의합니다"라고 말합니다. 3배 혹은 108배 또는 그 이상을 했든 간에, 마지막 절을 다 하고 일어나기 전에 다시 이마를 바닥에 대고 두 손을 받쳐 든 채 소원하는 바를 빌고 일어납니다.

5. Why do we bow to the Buddha image?
부처님께 절하는 이유

K: I was shocked to read a recent article that said that bowing is the third most popular form of practice among American Buddhists, after meditation and chanting.

F: Why does that strike you?

K: I didn't know that westerners would prostrate to show respect to someone or something. I thought they only shook hands or hugged.

F: Is that why many Korean buddhists bow to the Buddha image, is it to show respect?

K: It is our custom to bow to elders, teachers and parents to show respect and gratitude. So, of course we bow to the Buddha, the Great Teacher, as well! On top of that, bowing to the Buddha image is the same as bowing to myself, to my latent buddha-nature which everybody has inborn. Bowing is another way of practicing to find the true self, making myself humble. So, we've heard from monks that the more we bow, the more we rid ourselves of delusion and suffering. Just try it.

F: How many times do you bow at once?

K: It depends. 3-time-bow to the Buddha, Dharma and Sangha is basic, but it goes up to 1,000, 3,000 or more.

Most common is 108 bows on a daily basis. Today, 'the 108 prostrations of repentance (백팔참회)' has become popular with lay Buddhists. Just doing 108 bows gets you to sweat a lot and it makes you feel some toxins flush out of your body. Even non-buddhists come to know the effects of bowing when they want a fit body, but their bowing is a muscle exercise, while bowing of Buddhists is one of mindfulness practices. At the beginning of bowing practice, countless thoughts rise up, let them go and you should bring your attention to just bowing.

F: How do you count up to 108 or 1000 bows?

K: We use a prayer beads string, *yomju* in Korean. I'll get you one later.

K: 미국인 불자들 가운데서 절하는 것이 참선과 염불 수행에 이어 3위를 차지하고 있다는 최근 기사를 읽고 깜짝 놀랐어요.

F: 아니, 왜 깜짝 놀라요?

K: 난 서양사람들이 누군가에게 감사를 표하는 방법으로 절을 한다는 것을 상상도 못했어요. 그 사람들은 악수나 하고 포옹만 하는 줄 알았거든요.

F: 그럼 많은 한국 불자들이 부처님께 절을 하는 것이 감사와 존경을 표하기 때문입니까?

K: 나이든 분이나 선생님이나 부모님께 존경과 감사를 표할 때 절을 하는 것이 우리의 관습이지요. 그러니까 부처님께 절하는 것은 당연하지요. 게다가, 부처님께 절을 하는 것은 누구에게나 내

재되어 있는 내 안의 불성에게 절을 하는 겁니다. 그러니까 절은 나를 하심下心시키면서 진정한 자아를 찾는 또 다른 수행법이지요. 그래서 스님들이 절을 많이 하면 할수록 망상과 고통을 없애는 거라고 말씀하세요. 해봐요.

F: 절은 한 번에 몇 번이나 하는 건데요?

K: 그때그때 달라요. 불법승 삼보에 절하는 세 번은 기본이고요, 1,000번이나 3 000번, 그 이상도 할 수 있어요. 가장 흔하게는 매일 108배 수행을 하는 거지요. 요새는 대중적으로 108참회 기도를 많이 해요. 108배를 하면 땀을 많이 흘리게 되는데, 그때 몸 안 불순물이 빠져나간 것 같이 느껴져요. 비불자들도 체중조절에 절 수행의 효과를 잘 알고 있지만 그것은 근육 운동이고요. 불자들이 절하는 것은 정신 집중 수행의 하나예요. 절 수행 초기에는 수없이 많은 생각들이 떠올라요. 그럴 때 그런 생각에 따라가지 말고 절에만 집중해야 되요.

F: 108배 숫자를 어떻게 세지요?

K: 염주로 세요. 나중에 하나 사줄게요.

두 손을 포개고 고개만 살짝 숙이고 앉아서 하는 것이 고상한(?) 기도이고, 온몸으로 절을 하는 것은 기복이요 우상숭배로 몰아치는 사람들도 있지만, 절은 염불(recollecting Buddha's name/chanting), 간경(reading sutra) 주력(Dharani recitation) 등과 함께 기본적인 수행법이다. 해보지 않은 사람들이 어찌 그 맛을 알겠는가.

6. Prarer Beads: *Yomju*

염주念珠

In the word *Yomju*(Prayer Beads), yom means literally "recollect or have in mind", the same as in yombul(chanting). *Yomju* is a kind of assistant to help you to recollect the Buddha or the Bodhisattva in your mind all the time, keeping it as close as holding it in your hand.

It is not unusual for a lay buddhist to lead any ceremonial event striking a *Moktak* (wooden clacker) these days. However, this was denied until into the 1970s. Unlike *Moktak*, *Yomju* is the only thing that has been permitted for lay buddhists to possess from the time of the Buddha.

One story in the sutra goes that at the time of the Buddha, a minister of a small country came to the Buddha and said: "Blessed One, my country has suffered from drought and famine for many years. And I am tied up carrying out my tasks all year round. I would ask the Blessed One if there is any easy and useful way to practice for one like me who does not have enough time to cultivate myself following your teaching." The Blessed One spoke to him "Make a string with 108 soapberry tree seeds and chant the Buddha's name single-mindedly at any position — walking, abiding, sitting or lying. Chant using the beads on the string one by one up to 108 to make

Prayer Beads (*Yomju*), 염주

one round. When one million rounds are counted, the mind becomes concentrated and the body becomes tranquil. Then you will be liberated from the stream of birth and death and attain the unsurpassed way."

The figure 108 is the symbolic number of delusions that afflict humans. It comes from $6 \times 6 \times 3$. When our six sense organs: eyes, ears, nose, tongue, body and mind: come in contact with the six objects of the outer world: form, sound, smell, taste, matter and phenomena, this brings about 36 delusions. These 36 delusions throughout past, present, and future make 108 delusions.

Here is how to chant using 108 Prayer Beads, taught by the Great Master Ilta.

(translated by Brian Barry).
1. Sit comfortably, but with your back straight.
2. Hold your beads in your hands.
3. Put your palms together and bow once from the waist.
4. Repeat your wish three times (ex: "May Mother get well, May I pass my exam")
5. Take three or four slow, deep breaths. Now take one more deep breath, hold it, and take a gulp.
6. Begin chanting slowly three or four times and then pick up speed. Go faster and faster.
7. (When finished) Repeat your wish three times, put your palms together, and do another bow from the waist.

염주의 염솛은 '생각하다' 또는 '마음에 품다'의 뜻인데, 염불이란 단어에서도 같은 뜻이다. 염주는 불보살님의 명호를 부르며 기도드리거나 절 수행할 때 항시 손에 들고 하나씩 돌려 숫자를 세며 마음을 모으는 데 쓰는 불구佛具의 하나이다.

요즈음에는 재가자들이 목탁을 치며 예불이나 행사 진행을 하는 것이 전혀 이상스럽지 않지만 1970년대만 해도 이런 일은 거의 금기시하였다. 그러나 이러한 목탁과는 달리 염주는 부처님 당시부터 일반 재가자들이 지닐 수 있는 유일한 불구였다.

부처님 당시에 전해지는 얘기에 의하면, 어떤 작은 나라의 장관이 부처님께 와서 "세존이시여, 우리 왕국에 수년 째 가뭄이 들어 많은 사람들이 굶주리고 있습니다. 그래서 저는 일년 내내 일에 빠져 살고 있습니다. 저같이 수행하고 싶어도 시간을 낼 수 없는 사람이 할 수 있는 쉬운 수행법이 없습니까?" 하고 여쭈었다. 세존께서 말씀하셨다. "무환자나무 열매 108개에 줄을 꿰어서 행주좌와 시에 한마음으로 부처를 생각하며 염불을 하라. 한 번에 108개 염주 알을 돌리고 이렇게 100만 번을 돌리면 몸과 마음이 고요해질 것이고, 이로써 생사의 고통에서 벗어나 무상정등각을 이루리라."

108이란 숫자는 인간의 고통을 말하는 상징적 숫자인데 6×6× 3에서 나온 것이다. 눈, 귀, 코, 혀, 몸, 뜻의 여섯 감각기관이 객관세계의 여섯 경계인 색, 성, 향, 미, 촉, 법을 만나 36가지의 번뇌가 생기고, 이 번뇌가 과거, 현재, 미래의 삼세에 걸쳐서 108가지의 번뇌를 만든다.

일타 큰스님이 일러주시는 108염주 기도법을 소개하면,

① 척추를 곧추 세우고 편안한 자세로 앉는다.

② 손에 염주를 들고

③ 합장 반배를 한다.

④ 원하는 바(예를 들어, 어머니의 병세가 호전되기를, 시험에 합격하기를…)를 세 번 말한다.

⑤ 심호흡을 서너 번 고른 후 깊이 들이쉬고 내쉰 후

⑥ 불보살님 명호를 천천히 부르며 시작하다가 차츰 속도를 내어 집중한다.

⑦ 108염주를 다 돌렸으면 세 번 더 소원을 빌고, 합장 반배한다.

7. Mahayana (Great Vehicle): Bodhisattva Path
대승: 보살도

(in front of a painting of the Wisdom Dragon Ship)

F: Oh I easily recognize this painting as the Wisdom Dragon Ship (반야용선) you just told me about.

K: I think this painting expresses very well the notion of Mahayana Buddhism.

F: Mahayana? What is it?

K: Mahayana means great vehicle that can carry all beings from this shore of suffering to the other shore of liberation. Wouldn't it be nice if the vehicle is the greater, the better?

F: Sure it would.

K: Korea, China, Japan, and Vietnam are Mahayana Buddhist countries. Now we have a ship, and passengers, then what do we need to cross over this sea of suffering to reach our destination?

F: A captain, an able guide.

K: Yes, right. The Bodhisattva path appeared to meet this need. Bodhisattva is an ideal practitioner who vows to dedicate his whole life to the liberation of other beings, delaying his own enlightenment. The two most popular bodhisattvas in Korean Buddhism are Avalokiteshevara (관세음보살) and Ksitigarbha (지장보살). That's why most temples have separate halls for the two bodhisattvas to worship.

F: As you know, I have been to Sri Lanka. I haven't heard about bodhisattva there. Only the historical Sakyamuni Buddha is enshrined in the main hall.

K: It is because Sri Lanka is a Theravada Buddhists country. The Theravada Buddhism focuses on only personal liberation attaining arhatship, stressing keeping precepts.

F: Then what's the difference between Arhats and Buddha?

K: The First Arhats are the five disciples who attained Enlightenment on hearing the Buddha's First Teaching in Benares (Varanasi). The arhatship was degraded by Mahayana ideal to represent a lesser, selfish individual who strives only for personal liberation. We, in Mahayana, use the term 'Buddha' for a fully enlightened one.

(반야용선 그림 앞에서)

F: 이 그림이 방금 전에 얘기한 반야용선 그림인 줄 금방 알아보겠어요.

K: 이 그림이 대승불교 이념을 잘 표현하고 있다는 생각이에요.

F: 대승불교라니요? 뭐지요?

K: 마하야나란 많은 사람이 탈 수 있는 큰 수레란 뜻이죠. 차안此岸에서 피안彼岸에 이르려면 수레가 필요하지요. 그런데 그 수레가 크면 클수록 더 좋지 않을까요?

F: 그야 그렇지요.

K: 네. 한국 중국, 일본, 베트남 등이 대승불교국가죠. 자, 배도 있고 승객도 있으니까 이 고해의 바다를 건너려면 다음엔 뭐가 필요

Wisdom Dragon Ship, 반야용선(흥천사)

한가요?

F: 선장이요. 능력 있는 가이드가 있어야지요.

K: 그래서 보살도 정신이 생겼지요. 보살이란 자신의 성불을 늦추면서 중생 해탈의 서원을 발원한 이상적인 수행자를 말해요.

F: 내가 스리랑카에 갔던 것 알잖아요. 거기서는 보살이란 말을 못 들었어요. 법당에도 역사적인 부처님만 모시고 있어요.

K: 스리랑카는 남방불교 국가라 그래요. 남방불교는 계율을 중시하면서 아라한의 지위에 오르는 개인의 해탈에 초점을 맞추고 있기 때문에 역사적인 부처님만 모시고 있지요.

F: 그렇다면 아라한과 부처의 차이는 무엇입니까?

K: 첫 아라한들은 바라나시 녹야원에서 부처님의 초전 설법을 듣고 깨친 다섯 제자들이지요. 대승불교에서는 아라한을 개인의 해탈만을 위해 애쓰는 이기적인 각자覺者로 낮게 평가했어요. 대승불교에서는 부처라는 단어는 완전하게 깨달은 (무상 정등 정각) 분에게 써요.

8. Image of Buddhas and Bodhisattvas
부처와 보살의 상호

F: Frankly, I could not discern the differences between Buddha and Bodhisattva images. They look the same to me. How do you identify them?

K: I hear you. Same here when I was a beginner buddhist. Buddhas are always depicted as male, mostly wearing only monastic robes with the right shoulder uncovered. Bodhisattvas put on heavenly garments with many ornaments like crowns, earrings, bracelets, and necklaces that give them a feminine appearance.

F: Why are they described so differently? Aren't they both awakened ones?

K: Well. I can say that Bodhisattvas are on the way to the enlightenment, unlike the Buddha, who has reached the highest level of Enlightenment. Bodhisattvas are so sympathetic that they aspire to remain in the Saha world (samsara) and help beings in suffering, delaying their full enlightenment.

F: So bodhisattvas are depicted more favorably to human beings wearing many ornaments.

K: And besides, those splendid ornaments are signs of all kinds of merits that are acquired cultivating compassion

Avalokitesvara, 천수천안관세음보살(홍천사)

for others through countless lifetimes. The two most well-known Bodhisattvas in Korean faith is Avalokitesvara (Kwanseeum Bosal in Korean) and Ksitigarbha (Jijang Bosal). In larger temples they are worshipped in independent halls respectively. Avalokitesvara sometimes is depicted having a thousand hands and an eye on the end of each finger, which suits its Korean name, meaning one who observes the sounds of the world.

F: 솔직히 말해서 난 부처님과 보살님의 상호相好가 구별되지 않아요. 내겐 다 같아 보이거든요. 어떻게 구별하지요?

K: 이해해요. 나도 초심자였을 때 그랬어요. 부처님 상은 남성상에 편단우견(偏袒右肩; 가사를 오른쪽 어깨가 드러나보이게 입음)의 승복을 걸쳤지만 보살상은 많은 장식을 걸치고 있어요. 보관, 귀걸이, 팔찌, 목걸이 같은 거요.

F: 왜 그렇게 다르게 나타내죠? 두 분 다 깨달은 분이 아닌가요?

K: 이렇게 말하고 싶어요. 부처님은 최고의 경지에 오른 분이지만 보살은 그 길로 가는 분이지요. 다만 보살은 워낙 자비로워서 자신의 성불을 미루고 이 사바세계에 남아서 고통 받는 중생을 돕겠다고 서원을 세운 분이지요.

F: 그래서 인간들처럼 많은 장식물을 하고 있는 거군요.

K: 그렇죠. 그 아름다운 장식들은 수없는 생을 거치면서 자비수행을 한 결과로 얻은 공덕의 장엄물이라고 할 수 있어요. 한국 불자들한테 가장 잘 알려진 보살은 관세음보살과 지장보살이에요. 좀 규모 있는 큰 절에는 각각의 전각이 따로 있어요. 관세음보살은 때로 천수천안千手千眼 관세음보살로 모셔지는데, 세상의 소리를 관하는 분이라는 이름에 어울리는 모습이에요.

9. Mudras of the Buddha

수인手印

F: You said that the mudra is the unique hand gesture signifying will and powers of the Buddhas. The mudra of this Buddha image is quite different from others I've seen.

K: Yes, this is the 'Knowledge Fist mudra (지권인)', Virocana Buddha's mudra. This means the mundane world and Buddha's land are not two different places. The Virocana Buddha is known to be the embodiment of truth and knowledge.

F: Then what do you call the mudra of Sakyamuni Buddha?

K: We call it 'Calling the Earth Spirit to Witness mudra (항마촉지인)'. The story is that the Buddha called the spirit of the earth in order to witness his Enlightenment after defeating Mara's (evil spirit) temptation. So it is called 'subdue-demons mudra' as well. The index finger of the right hand over the right knee points to the earth and left hand positioned on the lap with palm up.

F: Do you mean that each Buddha image has its own different mudra?

K: Not always, but mudras can be a key to distinguishing between two similar Buddha images or paintings.

F: Very interesting. How about the Amitabha Buddha?

Knowledge Fist Mudra (Vairocana Buddha), 지권인 (비로자나불)

Calling the Earth Spirit Mudra (Sakyamuni Buddha), 항마촉지인 (석가모니불)

K: Actually, Amitabha's nine-grade mudra (9품인) is subtle and symbolic, representing 3 grades (품) of high, middle and low, and each grade has 3 existences (생) of high, middle and low rebirth in the Pure Land. I'd like to explain it while taking a look the paintings on the wall outside. Let's move.

(in front of the paintings) Please notice the position of the hands, and which fingers are touching the thumb-tips. This picture shows the highest existence in highest grade mudra of rebirth (상품 상생인), similar to samadhi mudra, touching thumbs and index fingers with both hands resting on the lap. In this case, the thumbs touch ring fingers; it represents the low existence in high grade (상품 하생). The middle grades (중품) are shown in this painting with both hands raised in the level of the chest, palms slightly outward. The thumbs touching middle fingers indicate 'middle grade, middle existence (중품 중생)'. The low grades (하품) show that the right or left hand is raised up to chest level with palm out and the other hand rests on the lap. The thumb-tips forming a circle with the other fingers is the same as we saw in high and middle grades.

F: 수인이란 부처님의 서원을 나타내는 독특한 손모양이라고 말했죠? 그런데 이 부처님의 수인은 여태껏 본 수인과 아주 다르네요.

K: 이것은 비로자나 부처님의 지권인이라고 해요. 부처와 중생이 둘이 아니라는 것을 상징해요. 비로자나 부처님은 진리의 화신으로 알려져 있죠.

F: 그럼 석가모니 부처님 수인은 뭐라고 하죠?

K: 항마촉지인이라고 해요. 부처님께서 정각을 이루시는 순간에 마왕의 유혹을 물리치고 부처님께서 지신을 불러 부처님의 정각을 증명케 한 것을 묘사한 거죠. 그래서 항마인이라고도 해요. 오른손 검지는 땅을 향하고 왼손은 손

Dispelling fear and Fulfilling-wishes
Mudra, 시무외 여원인

Highest grade, Highest existence Mudra   Low grade, middle existence Mudra
(Amitabha), 상품상생인 (아미타불)   (Amitabha), 하품중생인 (아미타불)

바닥을 위로 한 채 배꼽 부분 무릎 위에 놓는 거죠.

F: 그러면 부처님마다 각기 수인이 달라요?

K; 반드시 그렇지만은 않아요. 그러나 비슷한 부처님 상을 구별할
때 수인이 열쇠 말이 되기도 해요.

F: 재미있어요. 그럼 아미타불의 수인은 어떤가요?

K: 사실 아미타불의 9품 수인이 미묘하고 상징적이죠. 정토에 태어
날 때 상중하의 3품과 3생을 표현하고 있는데요. 밖에 벽화를 보
면서 설명하는 게 좋겠어요.

(벽화 앞에서) 자, 손이 놓여 있는 위치와 엄지가 어느 손가락과
맞닿는가를 잘 보세요. 이 그림은 상품 상생인으로, 두 손이 무릎
위에 있으면서 각각의 엄지가 검지와 만나고 있어요. 선정인과

Wall Painting of Amitabha's Nine grades Mudra, 9품 연화도 (흥국사)
(연화좌의 위치로 상·중·하품과 그에 따른 삼생의 수인을 표현하고 있다.)

비슷하지요. 만약 엄지가 약지와 만나고 있으면 상품 하생이라
고 합니다. 가운데 그림은 중품을 그리고 있어요. 중품은 약간 바
깥쪽을 향한 두 손이 모두 가슴 앞까지 올라가는데 엄지가 중지
와 닿고 있으니 중품 중생이 되겠지요. 하품을 나타낼 때는 한 손

은 치켜들고 다른 손은 무릎 위에 있어요. 엄지와 닿는 손가락으로 어느 생을 나타내고 있나 하는 것은 상품, 중품에서와 같아요.

대화가 단절된 곳에 다툼과 갈등이 있다고 말한다. 가정에서, 학교에서, 직장에서, 어디든 대화가 필요하다고 강조한다. 그러나 무언의 설법, 수인으로 우리에게 가르침을 펴고 계시는 불상을 대하면서 대화없이도 대화하는 그 경지를 새삼 헤아려보면 어떨까.

선정인 Samadhi Mudra / 전법륜인 Turning Dharma Wheel Mudra, 시무외 여원인 Dispelling fear and Fulfilling-wishes Mudra / 합장인 Putting Palms together Mudra / 천지인 Heaven and Earth Mudra, 아미타불 구품인 Amitabha's Nine grades Mudra.

10. Karma and Predestination

업과 숙명론

F: I wonder how you explain in Buddhism the problem of inequality in life. As you see all around you, bad people often receive respect and wield power, and many dishonest men live rich and luxurious lives. Sometimes an innocent child gets very sick and dies young.

K: As far as I know, most Christians do not wonder, accepting this inequality as the will of God, the Creator. But we Buddhists answer it by karma, the law of cause and effect.

F: Karma? I think I've heard of it.

K: Rebirth follows the law of karma, that is, beings are reborn according to the quality of their actions of past lives. Where appropriate karma, or causes and conditions are, rebirth will take place.

F: Do you mean our life is predestined?

K: It could be misunderstood like that. Many Koreans misuse this word karma in daily life as a retribution of whatever action. However, the word 'karma' means intentional actions. We put more importance on intention of the action rather than the behavior itself.

F: Then, if I happen to trample insects to death unintentionally, doesn't it generate karma?

K: No, the accidental action does not produce karma. Intentional actions matter. Karma can be changed by the efforts and actions in the present life. That's why we have to develop merits and cleansing our mind following the Buddha's teachings for a better life. Every moment, we are doing controlled by body, speech and mind, is not other than process of dying and being reborn.

F: 불교에서는 불평등의 문제를 어떻게 설명하는지 궁금해요. 주위에서 흔히 볼 수 있듯이 악인이 존경 받거나 권력을 휘두르고, 정직하지 않은 사람이 잘 살거나 죄 없는 어린애들이 병들어 일찍 죽는 일이 있잖아요.

K: 내가 알기로는 기독교인들은 이런 불공평을 신의 뜻으로 받아들이고 있지요. 그러나 우리 불자들은 인과법으로 설명해요.

F: 인과요? 들은 것 같아요.

K: 과거 생의 행위에 의한 인과에 따라 생을 받는 걸 말해요. 인연법에 따라 다시 몸을 받는다는 거죠.

F: 그렇다면 우리의 생은 이미 예정되어 있다는 건가요?

K: 그렇게 잘못 이해할 수도 있지요. 한국 사람들도 이 말을 '모든 행동에 대한 과보'로 잘못 쓰곤 해요. 그러나 카르마는 의도를 갖고 행한 행동을 말해요. 우리는 행위 그 자체보다도 행위의 동기에 더 중점을 두지요.

F: 그렇다면 내가 실수로 곤충을 밟았다면 인과가 안 일어나는 건가요?

K: 네. 우연한 행동은 인과를 안 만들어요. 의도적인 행동이 문제인 거죠. 인과는 현생의 노력으로 얼마든지 바뀔 수 있어요. 그렇기에 좀 더 나은 생을 위해 부처님 가르침에 따라 공덕을 쌓고 마음을 닦는 것이 필요한 거지요. 우리가 신구의 삼업에 의해 짓는 일상의 모든 순간들이 사실 나고 죽는(生死) 과정과 다르지 않아요.

Sow an act, reap a habit,

Sow a habit, reap a character,

Sow a character, reap a destiny.

행위가 습관이 되고, 습관이 성격을 만들어,

운명을 좌우한다

11. The Cycle of Rebirth: 6 Realms of Life
6도 윤회

How we think and act at this moment influences different results in the next moment. This is what we experience cause and effect in daily life. In fact, we go through the 6 realms of life more than dozens of times a day. In this sense, this 6 realms, where the cycle of rebirth takes place, can be interpreted as symbolic states of our mind.

In Buddhism, no one suffers eternal damnation. When their karmic accumulations, good or evil, are exhausted, the beings of that realm will be reborn in another 6 realms. Our goal as a buddhist is free from the cycle of rebirth.

1) Devas (Deities) Realm: The realm of happiness and long life, but the happiness is not permanent. When the good karma is run out, the Devas (Deities) fall from heaven and is reborn in another realms, mostly as a human. The role of beings in this realm is to guard the Buddha's teaching and protect the followers of them.

2) Human Realm: It is rare chances to be reborn in this realm that is considered as a desirable state to escape from the cycle of birth and death (samsara) by devoted cultivation. If anyone keeps on life cling to 'myself' and 'my family' without compassion or generosity for other beings, they are

none other than the life of animal state because any animals do exist and survive like that.

3) Asura Realm: The Asura is strong and powerful being and like to fighting. The karma of hate, jealousy and lust for power causes rebirth in this realm.

4) Hungry Ghosts Realm: They are constantly unsatisfied spirits with large stomach and tiny throat. Strong attachments, greed and obsession are the rebirth causes of this realm.

5) Hell Realm: There are many hells like 8 hot hells, 8 cold hells, and many more. Anger and cruelty cause rebirth in this Hell Realm.

6) Animal Realm: This realm is conditioned by stupidity, prejudice and ignorance.

In Buddhism, we do speak of rebirth, not incarnation. Because Buddhism denies a substantial entity, permanent Self (Atman) that makes reincarnation. Buddhists' concept is that beings are nothing but a combination of 5 aggregates (matter, feeling, perception, mental formation and consciousness) that are constantly changing with cause and conditions. This is the basic of 'no-self thought' in Three Dharma Seals of Buddha's teaching.

우리가 이 순간에 생각하고 행동하는 것의 결과는 다음 순간에 바로 나타난다. 이것이 바로 인과를 일상에서 경험하는 일인데, 사실상 우리는 하루에도 수십 번 6도 윤회를 하는 셈이다. 이런 의미에서 6도 윤회는 우리들 마음의 상태를 나타내는 상징적인 설명이라고 할 수 있다.

불교에서는 영원히 지옥에서 고통받고 사는 일은 없다고 말한다. 선업이든 악업이든 그 업력이 다하면 6도 중에 다른 곳의 몸을 받는다고 한다. 불자로서의 우리의 목표는 이러한 윤회의 고리를 끊는 것이다.

1) 천상계: 행복과 장수가 보장된 곳이긴 하지만 영원한 곳은 아니다. 이곳 중생도 선업이 소진되면 6도 중 하나에 태어나는데 대개 사람 몸을 받는다. 천상계 중생들의 역할은 불법을 수호하고 수행자들을 보호하는 일이다.

2) 인간계: 열심히 수행정진하면 윤회의 고리를 끊을 수 있는 가장 바람직한 곳이라는 의미에서 인간의 몸을 받는 것이 쉬운 일은 아니라고 한다. 다른 사람들에 대한 배려와 자비심이 없이 나와 내 가족에만 집착하여 사는 것은 인간이면서도 축생의 삶과 다를 바가 없다.

3) 아수라계: 아수라는 힘이 세고 강력해서 싸우기를 좋아하며, 증오, 질투, 권력욕이 강하면 이곳에 태어난다고 한다.

4) 아귀계: 위장은 크지만 목구멍이 하도 작아서 항상 굶주림에 시달리는 중생계. 탐심이 강하고 강한 집념이 아귀계에 태어나는 원인이 된다.

5) 지옥계: 8열 지옥, 8한 지옥과 같이 무수한 지옥이 있다고 한다. 분심이 많거나 잔인함이 강하면 이곳의 몸을 받는다.

6) 축생계: 어리석거나 편견이 심하거나 무명에 찌들면 축생계에

The Cycle of Rebirth, 육도윤회

떨어진다.

불교에서는 환생이란 말 대신에 다시 태어남(재생)이라고 한다. 이는 불교는 아트만과 같이 불멸하는 실체가 있어 윤회하면서 환생을 한다고 보지 않기 때문이다. 인간을 5온(색수상행식)의 결합으로 원인과 조건(인연)에 의해 끊임없이 변하는 존재로 보기 때문이다. 이는 삼법인의 하나인 무아사상의 기본이다.

무아(No-self)인데 무엇이 윤회하느냐는 질문을 받곤 했다. 이는 현상계에서의 변화가 똑같지는 않으면서 계속해서 비슷하게 변화되기(相續) 때문에 자아가 윤회한다는 착각을 하게 되는 속제(俗諸, Conventional Truth)에 묶인 질문이다. 고정불변의 실체가 없고 항상하는 것이 없기 때문에 인연이 모이면 서로 다른 조건에 의존하면서 생멸하는 연기적 존재임을 깊이 생각하면 '무엇이 윤회하는가'의 의문은 이 무아윤회로 자연스럽게 풀리지 않을까.

12. Principle of Dependent Origination
연기설: 법화경 화성유품 중에서

"Then he (the Great Universal Wisdom Excellent Thus Come One) broadly expounded the Law of the twelve-linked chain of causation: ignorance causes action, action causes consciousness, consciousness causes name and form, name and form cause the six sense organs, the six sense organs cause contact, contact causes sensation, sensation causes desire, desire causes attachment, attachment causes existence, existence causes birth, birth causes old age and death, worry and grief, suffering and anguish. If ignorance is wiped out, then action will be wiped out. If action is wiped out, then consciousness will be wiped out. If consciousness is wiped out, then name and form will be wiped out. If name and form are wiped out, then the six sense organs will be wiped out. If the six sense organs are wiped out then contact will be wiped out. If contact is wiped out, then sensation will be wiped out. If sensation is wiped out, then desire will be wiped out. If desire is wiped out, then attachment will be wiped out. If attachment is wiped out, then existence will be wiped out. If existence is wiped out, then birth will be wiped out. If birth is wiped out, then old age and death, worry and grief, suffering and anguish will be wiped out."

- from The Parable of the Phantom City in The Lotus Sutra
  translated by Burton Watson -

"그리고 대통지승여래께서는 널리 십이 인연법을 설하셨느니라. 즉 무명이 조건이 되어 행이 있게 되고, 행이 조건이 되어 인식하게 되며, 인식이 조건이 되어 명색이 생기고, 명색이 조건이 되어 여섯 군데 인식기관이 생겨나며, 여섯 군데 인식기관이 조건이 되어 접촉하게 되고, 접촉이 조건이 되어 느낌이 생기며, 느낌이 조건이 되어 갈애가 생기고, 갈애가 조건이 되어 집착이 생기며, 집착이 조건이 되어 생존에 대한 본능이 생기게 되고, 생존에 대한 본능이 조건이 되어 태어나게 되며, 태어남이 조건이 되어 늙고 죽음으로 인한 근심과 슬픔 등 갖가지 고통들이 생겨나게 되느니라. 따라서 무명이 없어지면 곧 행이 사라지고, 행이 없어지면 인식이 사라지며, 인식이 없어지면 명색이 사라지고, 명색이 없어지면 여섯 군데 인식기관이 사라지며, 여섯 군데 인식기관이 없어지면 접촉이 사라지고, 접촉이 없어지면 느낌이 사라지며, 느낌이 없어지면 갈애가 사라지고, 갈애가 없어지면 집착이 사라지며, 집착이 없어지면 생존에 대한 본능이 사라지고, 생존에 대한 본능이 없어지면 태어남이 사라지며, 태어남이 없어지면 늙고 죽음으로 인한 근심과 슬픔 등 온갖 고통들이 사라지게 되느니라."

-『법화경』화성유품 중에서:『우리말 법화경』/ 혜조 스님 번역 -

13. Why so many Buddhas and Bodhisattvas?
많은 부처와 보살은 왜?

K: You've looked around the temple compound. What's your impression? Do you have any questions?

F: Thanks a lot for your explanations so far. Well, I saw many Buddhas and Bodhisattvas Images in different shrines. I wonder if one Buddha image isn't enough to deliver Buddha's teaching. You told me that the nature of Buddha and sentient being is the same though.

K: Good question! Although every sentient being has the same Buddhahood, their level of understanding and believing in Buddha's teaching vary depending on the individual's spiritual capacities and wishes. This is preached well in the Medicinal Herbs in the Lotus Sutra. If I need to develop compassion, I recollect on Avalokiteshvara Bodhisattva, and when I pray for the deceased I call for Ksitigarbha Bodhisattva. To meet various needs, Buddhas or Bodhisattvas appear in different forms and situations to help us in various ways. Each Buddha and Bodhisattva has his own vows, how they practice and inspire us, that show us we could become a buddha through constant devotional cultivation.

부처와 보살은 왜 많은가

K: 절 경내를 돌아보았는데 느낌이 어때요? 질문 있어요?

F: 설명 잘 들었습니다. 그런데 전각마다 다른 부처님과 보살님들
이 있던데요. 부처님 한 분으로는 가르침을 다 전할 수 없어서 그
런 건가요. 부처와 중생이 같다라고 말하지 않았나요?

K: 좋은 질문이에요. 중생은 누구나 불성을 갖고 있긴 하지만 근기
가 다르고 그에 따른 바람이 다르지요. 예를 들어 자비가 필요할
때는 관음보살을 염하고, 죽은 사람을 위해서는 지장보살께 기
도하지요. 이렇게 불보살님들은 다양한 방법과 여러 가지 모습
으로 중생들과 교류하는 겁니다. 그들이 어떻게 수행하였는가를
보여주고, 궁극에는 우리 중생도 끊임없이 정진하면 부처가 될
수 있다는 것을 보여주는 겁니다.

14. Medicinal Herbs

법화경 약초유품 중에서

……

The Buddha's undifferentiating preaching
Is, like the rain, of a single flavor,
In accord with the beings' natures
Differently received,
Just as what those grasses and trees
Receive is in every case different.

……

In this way, O Kasyapa,
Is the Dharma preached by the Buddha
To be likened to a great cloud,
Which with the rain of a single flavor
Moistens human flowers,
Enabling each to perfect it fruit.
Kasyapa, let it be known
That, when by invoking causes and conditions
And a variety of parables
I demonstrate the Buddha Path,
This is my expedient device.
The other Buddhas are also this way.

Now, for your sakes,

I preach the most true Reality:

The multitude of voice-hearers

Have in no wise crossed over to extinction.

What you are now treading

Is the bodhisattva-path.

By the gradual cultivation of learning,

You shall all achieve Buddhahood.

　　– from the Scripture of the Lotus Blossom of the Fine Dharma

　　　translated by Leon Hurvitz –

법화경 약초유품 (부분)

(……)

부처님의 평등한 설법

똑같은 맛의 비와 같으나,

중생의 성품에 따라서 받아들여짐이 다르나니

초목들이 똑같은 비를 맞고도 자라남이 다른 것과 같도다.

(……)

이와 같이 가섭아,

부처님의 설법은

큰 구름이 똑같은 맛의 비로써

사람들의 꽃을 적시어 각각 열매 맺게 하는 것과 같도다.

가섭아, 마땅히 잘 명심하여라.

여러 인연들과 갖가지 비유로써

불도를 열어 보이나니

이는 나의 방편이자 다른 부처님들도 마찬가지니라.

이제 너희들을 위하여

가장 참된 진실을 말하건대

여러 성문대중들은

모두 진짜 열반을 얻은 것이 아니니라.

너희들이 닦아야 할 바는

바로 보살도이니

점점 닦아 배워 나간다면

모두 마땅히 성불하리라.

- 『우리말 법화경』 / 혜조 스님 번역 -

Directly, then, or indirectly,

All I do will be for others' benefit.

And solely for their sake, I dedicate

My actions for the gaining of enlightenment.

직접적이든 간접적이든

내가 하는 모든 일은 중생의 행복을 위한 일입니다.

깨달음을 얻기 위한 모든 나의 헌신은 온전히 그들을 위한 것입니다.

(Shantideva의 Happiness Lessons 중에서)

15. Six Offerings to the Buddha

육법공양

F: I'll tell you what, I bought a bunch of incense at Insa-dong yesterday.

K: Why incense? There are so many things that make you curious. aren't there?

F: Yes, there are. I just like its fragrance.

K: In fact, incense is one of the six offerings to the Buddha.

F: I didn't know that. What are the others?

K: Besides incense, they are rice or sometimes rice cakes, flowers, fruits, tea or pure water, and candles.

F: Ah, now I see why there are so many kinds of fruits, flowers, and Korean rice cakes on the main altar in the Main Buddha Hall.

K: These offerings represent the six paramitas or perfections. They are means for practice by Buddhists to cross over from this shore of the secular world to the other shore of nirvana. They are giving, holding precepts, endurance, effort, concentration and wisdom.

F: 있잖아요. 나 어제 인사동에서 향 샀어요.

K: 왜 향을 샀어요? 인사동에는 별별 것이 많은데, 안 그래요?

F: 그렇긴 해요. 그냥 향기가 좋아서 샀어요.

K: 사실은 향은 부처님께 드리는 6법 공양물 중 하나지요.

F: 그래요? 몰랐어요. 그럼 나머지는 뭔데요?

K: 향 이외에 쌀, 꽃, 과일, 차와 초 혹은 등이에요. 쌀은 떡으로 올리기도 하고 차 대신에 물을 올리기도 해요.

F: 아 그래서 법당 상단에 보면 많은 과일들하고 떡하고 꽃들이 있었군요.

K: 이 여섯 공양물을 육바라밀과 연계해서 설명하기도 해요. 육바라밀은 차안에서 피안에 이르기 위한 여섯 가지 실천 덕목을 말하는 것인데 보시, 지계, 인욕, 정진, 선정, 지혜를 말해요.

쌀은 육신을 먹이고 (보시/donation), 향은 스스로를 태우고 (지계/precepts), 한 송이 꽃이 피기까지 많은 정성 (인욕/endurance)이 필요하고, 열매 맺음에는 부단한 노력 (정진/effort)이 요구되고, 차는 선정 (concentration), 촛불(등)은 광명으로 모든 것을 환하게 해주는 지혜(wisdom)로 비유, 설명된다.

16. Bathing the Baby Buddha
관불

F: Why are those people standing in line over there?

K: They are going to bathe the baby Buddha.

F: What do you mean?

K: It's an annual event on the Buddha's birthday. It originated from the legendary tale that when the Buddha was born, two dragons appeared to wash him with warm fragrant water.

F: That reminds me of baptism in the Baptist Church.

K: In the sense of purification, I think, it is the same. Won't you join them? While doing it, make this vow: "now that I pour pure water on Tathagata's head, I will try to cultivate my body and mind all the more to reach the goal of supreme awakening."

F: Dragons represent evil things in western countries, you know?

K: I know it, but in Buddhism it is one of eight guardians which protect the Buddha and his teachings. You will see many pictures of dragons at a temple, for instance, on the base of a stone monument, a carved dragon for loop on top of the Dharma bell, or on the roof and a painting of wisdom dragon ship.

Bathing the Baby Buddha, 관불

F: 저기에 왜 사람들이 줄을 서 있나요?

K: 애기 부처님을 씻겨 드리려고 그래요.

F: 무슨 소리죠?

K: 부처님오신날에만 하는 연중행사지요. 부처님 탄생 시에 두 마
   리의 용이 나타나서 따뜻한 물로 씻겨드렸다는 설화에서 유래했
   대요.

F: 침례교의 세례의식이 생각나네요.

K: 정화라는 의미에서는 같다고 생각해요. 같이 해볼래요? 이런 생
   각을 하면서 해봐요.
   "제가 지금 여래의 머리에 물을 부으니 정각에 이르도록 더욱 더
   정진하겠습니다."

F: 서양에서는 용이 악을 상징하는 거 알아요?

K: 네. 그러나 불교에서는 부처님과 그 가르침을 외호하는 팔부신 중의 하나지요. 절에 있는 돌비석 기단이나 범종의 용뉴나 지붕에, 또 반야용선 그림 등에서 용무늬를 많이 볼 수 있을 겁니다.

부처님께서는 업력(karmic power)으로 태어나는 우리 중생들과 달리 헤아릴 수 없는 과거세로부터의 선근 공덕(virtuous quality)과 원력(will/vow power)으로 우리에게 오셨습니다. 부처님오신날, 관불을 하며 여래(Tathagata) 응공(Worthy) 정변지(Omniscient) 명행족(Possessed of Wisdom and Practice), 선서(Well-gone), 세간해(Knower of the World), 무상사(Unsurpassed One), 조어장부(Tamer of Men), 천인사(Master of God and Men), 불세존(World Honored One)으로 오신 뜻을 다시금 새겨봅니다.

Above and below the heavens,

I alone, am high and noble.

With entire world mired in sufferings,

I will bring peace to the world.

(천상천하 유아독존 삼계개고 아당안지)
天上天下 唯我獨尊 三界皆苦 我當安之

17. The Meaning of Lotus Lantern
연등

F: Colorful lanterns filled the temple yard. Amazing!

K: We are celebrating the Buddha's Birthday. As I told you, a lantern or candle is one of six offerings to the Buddha.

F: I saw white lanterns over there too.

K: Those are for the dead, while colorful lanterns are for the living beings. We count white lotuses so superior that we offer white lanterns to the dead. The lotus flower is a symbol of Buddhism. It grows up through the muddy, dirty water but the flowers blossom unsoiled. Some say that flower symbolizes enlightenment while the root, the world of sentient beings. And some say that since a lotus bears fruit and flower at the same time, that shows the law of cause and effect.

K: By the way, do you have any plans this Sunday?

F: Nothing special. Why?

K: There will be a Lotus Lantern Festival on Jongno Street. There, you can make a lotus lantern by yourself and carry it in the lantern parade at night. How does that sound?

F: Sounds good! But why a lotus-shaped lantern?

K: Lotus lanterns symbolize wisdom. Wisdom and compassion are two essentials to attain enlightenment. When you light a lantern, darkness flees away. Likewise, if you light your mind with wisdom, your delusion will disappear.

F: 절 마당에 화려한 등이 하나 가득이네요.

K: 부처님 오신 날을 봉축하는 거예요. 말했듯이 등(촛불)은 여섯 가지 공양물 중 하나예요.

F: 저쪽에는 흰색등도 있군요.

K: 흰색등은 조상(죽은 자)을 위한 것이고, 색등은 산 자를 위한 겁니다. 백련을 최고로 치기 때문에 흰색등은 조상을 위해 달아요. 불교의 상징 꽃이 연꽃이죠. 연꽃은 더러운 흙탕물 속에서 자라지만 꽃은 아름답지요. 그래서 꽃은 깨달음을, 뿌리는 중생을 말하기도 해요. 또 연꽃은 꽃과 열매가 동시에 열리는 것이 인과의 법칙을 보이는 거라고도 해요.

K: 그런데 이번 일요일에 뭐 할 거예요?

F: 특별한 일이 없는데요. 왜요?

K: 종로에서 연등축제가 있어요. 연등도 만들고 밤에는 내가 만든 연등을 들고 제등행렬에 참가할 수 있어요. 해볼래요?

F: 근사할 것 같군요. 그런데 왜 연꽃 등이죠?

K: 연등은 지혜를 상징해요. 자비와 지혜는 성불하는 데 기본 요소지요. 등을 켜면 어둠이 도망가듯이 내 마음에 지혜의 등을 켜면 번뇌가 사라지는 것을 상징하지요..

부처님오신날이 되면 연중행사니까, 혹은 누구나 다니까, 별 생각 없이 등을 달지는 않는지. 등불이 주변을 밝게 하듯이 나도 지혜의 등불을 밝혀, 응무소주 이생기심(You should arouse your mind without being attached to anything)의 가르침을 따라 집착을 버리는 연습을 꾸준히 하겠다는 서원을 세워보는 것은 어떨까?

Lotus Lantern,
연등(조계사)

18. Memorial Rituals for 49 Days

천도재/ 49재

F: I've heard that Korean Buddhists hold memorial periods for 49 days when someone dies.

K: The services are given 7 times, every seventh day. The dead are judged every seven days to be assigned a new life in one of the six realms: hell, ghosts, animals, asura, human or celestial beings (gods or devas). Buddhists believe in rebirth. Their next life is determined by the actions in this life. They remain in an intermediate state for 49 days.

F: Ah! That is why it requires 49 days of prayer.

K: It is during these 49 days that the dead still have a strong link with this life. Therefore, their family members' heartfelt and sincere praying for them can be influential to their better rebirth. The ritual can give the dead a chance to repent of all misdeeds and have a change of heart, aspiring to be reborn in the Pure Land. Usually we read the Formless Precepts (무상계) and Diamond Sutra (금강경) for the dead. Those are teachings of emptiness of things or non-attachment of life. This ritual is actually for the living rather than for the dead, I think.

F: What? Why is that?

K: A painful sense of loss might be cured over these ritual

periods. This was my story when my mother passed away some years ago, I started reading the Diamond Sutra for her but it ended up soothing and cleansing me in the end.

F: 한국 불자들은 누군가 죽으면 49일 동안 애도 기간을 지킨다는 얘기를 들었어요.

K: 매 7일마다 일곱 번 재를 지내지요. 바로 그날마다 6도 중에 어디에 태어나는가를 재판받는답니다. 6도는 지옥, 아귀, 축생, 아수라, 인간, 하늘을 말합니다. 불교는 다음 생을 믿거든요. 다음 생은 이생에서의 행위에 의해 결정된다고 해요. 49일 동안을 중음의 상태에 있는 거지요.

F: 아, 그래서 49일 기도가 필요한 거군요.

K: 그동안에는 죽은 사람이 살아 있는 사람과 강한 유대를 아직 갖고 있대요. 그래서 후손들이 좋은 곳에 태어나게 정성껏 기도를 하는 겁니다. 이런 의식을 통해서 망자가 잘못을 뉘우치고 생에 미련을 버리고 마음을 바꿔 정토에 가겠다는 마음을 내도록 도와 줄 수 있다는 거지요. 그래서 주로 영가들께 「무상계」와 『금강경』을 많이 읽어줍니다. 다 공의 가르침에 관한 겁니다. 사실 이런 의식은 죽은 사람보다도 산 사람을 위한 것 같아요.

F: 뭐라고요? 왜죠?

K: 가족을 잃은 상실감이 이 기간에 나도 모르게 치유되는 것 같았어요. 내 경험에서 하는 말이에요. 어머니가 돌아가셨을 때 49재를 지내면서 어머니를 위해서 매일 금강경을 읽어드렸는데, 결

국은 그것이 내게 위안을 주는 것은 물론이고 마음이 정화되는
걸 느꼈거든요.

We beg that the merit gained through these gifts

May be spread far and wide to everyone,

So that we and other living beings be reborn in the Land of Bliss

Behold the holy face of Amitabha Buddha

May attain the Buddha Way all together

원하옵건대 이 공덕이 온누리에 두루하여

저와 함께 중생들이 극락정토 태어나서

무량수불 친견하고 모두 성불하여지이다.

願以此功德 普及於一切 我等與衆生

當生極樂國 同見無量壽 皆共成佛道

19. All Spirits' Day: Ullambana Day
백중(百中)

K: Today is 'All spirits day', *Baekjung* in Korean, counted one of 4 anniversaries of Korean Buddhist culture.

F: What are the others?

K: They are Buddha's birthday as you know this well, Enlightenment day (the 8th day in December), Renunciation day (8th day in February) and Parinirvana (Passing away) day (15th day in February) by lunar calendar.

F: What are those white papers sticking all over the wall?

K: They are paper soul tablets. The names of the dead are written on them.

F: Do people bow to the deceased?

K: Yes, they do. Now we are in the 49 memorial periods for the ancestors until the full moon day of seventh month by lunar calendar, the last day of summer retreat.

F: Any meaning on the last day of retreat?

K: Yes. This tradition can be traced back to the time of the Buddha. Moggallana, a close disciple of the Buddha got to know that his mother was suffering at the Hungry Ghosts Realm. He asked the Buddha if there was anything he could do to save his mother. The Buddha told him to make offerings of plenty of food to the assembly of the sangha on the last day of retreat. Then the virtuous merits from offerings would transfer to the deceased ancestors. As the same tradition has been kept in Korean monastery, while the meditation monks are seeking their *Hwadu*, other monks and laity make offerings to their ancestors and praying to help them rid of ignorance.

K: 오늘은 한국불교에서 4대 명절 중 하나로 꼽는 백중날이에요.

F: 나머지 명절은 무엇인데요?

K: 당신도 잘 아는 부처님오신날(4월 8일)과 성도절(12월 8일), 출가절(2월 8일), 열반절(2월 15일)이지요. 전부 음력이에요.

F: 저기 벽에 가득 붙어 있는 흰 종이들은 뭐지요?

K: 위패를 모신 종이예요. 종이에는 죽은 조상들의 이름이 적혀 있어요.

F: 그럼 저 사람들은 죽은 조상들에게 절을 하는 겁니까?

K: 네, 음력 7월 보름까지 우리가 49일 동안 조상님들을 위해 기도하는 추모기간이지요.

F: 그날이 무슨 의미 있는 날이에요?

K: 네 그래요. 부처님 당시에 제자 중 목련존자가 자기 어머니가 아귀가 되어 고통받고 있는 것을 알게 되었어요. 목련존자는 부처님께 어머님을 구할 수 있는 방법을 여쭈었고, 부처님께서는 안거 해제일에 백 가지 음식을 준비해서 승가 스님들께 공양 올리면 그 공덕으로 어머니를 구할 수 있다고 했어요. 그와 같은 전통

이 그대로 한국불교에서도 살아 있어서, 선방 스님들이 화두 참구에 정진할 때 다른 스님들과 재가불자들은 공양물을 준비하고 조상님들이 무명에서 벗어나길 바라는 기도를 (49일 동안) 드립니다.

As long as space endures,

As long as there are beings to be found,

May I continue likewise to remain

To drive away the sorrows of the world.

허공계가 다하고 중생계가 다할지라도

오늘 세운 이 서원 끝없사오리

Part 2
Outside the Compound

1. What is a Temple?

절이란?

K: Shall we go to a Korean buddhist temple today?

F: Sounds good. Is it a place like church?

K: A buddhist temple is a place where the Buddha is enshrined, and various religious ceremonies are held. Buddhists show respects to the Buddha and pray for bliss for their family and what they wish for. Above all, monks actually live there and cultivate wisdom and compassion for the four-fold assembly.

F: Is there anything interesting there?

K: You will find unique Korean traditions of Buddhist arts such as paintings, sculptures, and buildings, as well as Buddha's Teaching.

F: Then the temple is in the city, near here?

K: Most famous temples are deep in the mountains. As you may know, Buddhism was suppressed during the last Joseon dynasty. So monastic communities had to move to the mountains to survive. Ironically, that helped Korean Buddhism keep tradition alive up to now. Today, many temples have been revived in the cities providing daily chanting services, and various programs for all ages, like studying sutra, practicing meditation, praying overnight,

Haeinsa Temple, 해인사 가람

and pilgrimages to the great temples.

K: 우리 오늘 절에 가볼까요?

F: 그래요. 그런데 거긴 교회 같은 곳인가요?

K: 부처님을 모시고 종교적인 행사와 함께 절하고 기도드리는 곳이
   죠. 불자들은 부처님께 예배드리며 가족의 행복과 소원을 빌고,
   스님들은 그곳에 살면서 사부대중과 함께 지혜와 자비 수행을
   하는 곳이기도 하지요.

F: 재미있는 게 있어요?

K: 한국의 그림, 조각, 건축 같은 것을 볼 수 있을 뿐 아니라 부처님
   의 가르침을 들을 수 있어요.

F: 그럼 여기서 가까워요?

K: 유명한 사찰들은 깊은 산중에 있지요. 알겠지만 지난 마지막 왕조 조선에서는 억불을 했기 때문에 절이 산으로 갈 수밖에 없었어요. 그런데 역설적이게도 그랬기 때문에 오늘날까지 한국불교의 전통을 간직할 수 있답니다. 요새는 다시금 도시에 사찰이 많이 생겨서 불자들한테 다양한 프로그램을 제공해요. 예를 들어 매일 예불은 물론이고 경전 공부, 참선 실수, 철야 기도, 사찰 순례 등이지요.

절하다는 prostrate이라는 표현과 함께 bow의 쉬운 말도 있고, pay/show respect to the Buddha로 번역하기도 한다. 염불하다는 recollect Buddha's name 혹은 쉽게 chant/recite를 쓰기도 한다. 불상은 Buddha statue/image로 쓰는데 statue보다는 image를 권한다. 사부대중(four-fold assembly)은 비구, 비구니, 우바이, 우바새를 가리킨다.

2. Flagpole Supports
당간지주

In the old days, it was a fluttering flag called *dang and* the lofty flagpole *danggan* that we met first on the way to a temple before reaching the one pillar gate. A flag was hung to be seen from far away, indicating the boundaries of the temple and the big event that was going to take place on a special day. To support this lofty iron or wooden standing flagpole there were huge pillars made of stone called *Danggan Jiju*. Today, most poles are gone through Japanese colonial plunder or the Korean War, but two stone pillars alone are mostly found at the ruins of old temples, lonely but majestic yet. Here was the actual starting point of the journey to the sacred realm, Buddha's land.

'여기서부터 사찰 영역입니다'라고 표시하는 당(깃발)을 높이 걸기 위해 높직한 당간(당을 다는 기둥/찰간)을 만들고 그것을 지지해 주는 버팀목이 당간지주인데, 오늘날에는 주인공인 당과 당간이 일제 때 공출과 한국 전쟁 중의 피해로 자취를 감추고 지주만이 남아 있다. 지금은 도심사찰에서는 말할 것도 없고 산중사찰에서도 당간지주를 만나기는 쉽지 않다. 이제는 완전히 도심이 되어 버린 주택

가 한가운데에서 생뚱맞게 철책으로 보호 받고 있는 당간 지주를
어쩌다 마주치면 반갑기보다 안타깝다. 애초부터 당간지주를 보러
가는 폐사지 탐방이 오히려 마음이 가볍다. 세월의 자취를 간직한
채 의연히 서 있는 당간지주를 대하며 나도 모르게 숙연해진다.

Flagpole Supports,
당간지주(굴산사지)

3. One Pillar Gate

일주문

K: This is the first gate of a temple called the One Pillar Gate, usually placed far below the temple. In the case of a mountain temple, from here there is some walking, a winding path up to the main temple compound.

F: Did you say that this is the 'One Pillar Gate'?

K: Yes, I did.

F: But there seems to be two pillars actually.

K: You are right. Usually a roof covers four pillars, one for each of the cardinal directions. But the roof of this gate has two pillars. (moving to the side of the gate) If you see here on each side, it seems to have only one pillar.

F: Oh, that's interesting. Is there any special reason to call this gate one pillar?

K: There sure is. One pillar symbolizes one mind. Here, you let go of worldly worries and try to gather your single mind vowing to strive to awakening. The wooden signboard under the eaves tells us the temple name and the name of the mountain where the temple is located.

F: I see, there are no doors, even though you call it a gate. Is it open to anybody?

K: Yes, you are more than welcome to visit a temple in Korea.

One Pillar Gate, 일주문 (용암사)

K: 이 문이 절에 들어가는 첫째 관문인 일주문이에요. 보통 절이 있
   는 산 훨씬 밑에 있어서 절까지는 꼬불거리는 산길을 한참 걸어
   올라가야 하지요.

F: 이 문을 일주문이라 한다고 했어요?

K: 네, 그랬어요.

F: 그렇지만 기둥이 두 개가 있잖아요.

K: 맞아요. 대개 지붕은 네 개의 기둥 위에 있는 법이지만 이 문은
   두 개의 기둥 위에 지붕을 얹혔어요. (문 옆쪽으로 움직이며) 이쪽
   에 와서 보면, 마치 기둥이 한 개만 있는 것처럼 보여요.

F: 재미있네요. 이렇게 짓고 부르는 특별한 이유라도 있어요?

K: 그럼요. 일심을 상징하거든요. 여기서부터는 세상의 걱정거리를

버리고 깨달음의 길로 나아가겠다는 일심이지요. 처마 밑 간판
에는 절이 있는 산의 이름과 절 이름을 써 놓아요.

F: 큰 문이라면서 출입문이 없네요. 누구나 들어오라는 겁니까?

K: 그렇지요. 한국 절은 누구든 환영하지요.

일주문을 single beam gate라고도 한다. 일주문은 불국정토(Buddha's
pure land)와 세속(secular world)을 가르는 경계선이라는 상징적 의미이
다. 이 경계를 지나 불국토로 향하는 마음자세는 부처님 법을 믿고, 따
르고, 종국에는 성불하겠다는 일심이 되어야겠다.

일주문 기둥에는 대개 입차문래 막존지해(入此門來 莫存知解: When
you enter from this gate, you should discard everything you've known.)
라고 쓰여 있다.

입차문래 막존지해, 북한산 상원사

4. Four Guardians' Gate

사천왕문

K: This is the second gate, the Four Guardians' Gate. Four heavenly kings are here. Sometimes it is called the Diamond Gate.

F: They look very scary.

K: At first glance they might be scary, but if you look carefully, you will find that they are smiling.

F: Why are they here?

K: Each heavenly king takes charge of one of the 4 cardinal directions to protect Buddha and his teaching. They were gods of Hindu origin, but they became buddhist guardians to keep away evil spirits after listening to the Buddha's teaching. The things they are holding differ slightly depending on temples.

F: Oh, I notice that the guardian who is holding a musical instrument is smiling.

K: Yes, he is the guardian of the east, and is singing happily after he listened to the Buddha's teaching.

K: 여기는 두 번째 문인 사천왕문이에요. 사천왕을 모셔놓았지요. 때로는 금강문이라고도 해요.

F: 굉장히 무서워 보이는데요.

K: 첫눈에는 그렇게 보여도 자세히 보면 얼굴에 웃음이 있어요.

F: 사천왕들은 왜 여기 있지요?

K: 그들은 동서남북 사방을 지키면서 부처님 법을 수호하는 일을
   합니다. 원래는 힌두의 신이었으나 부처님 말씀을 듣고 수호신
   이 되어 나쁜 기운이 들어오지 못하도록 막고 있지요. 사천왕의
   지물持物은 절마다 조금씩 달라요.

F: 저기 악기를 들고 있는 천왕이 정말 웃고 있네요.

K: 맞아요. 동쪽을 지키는 지국천왕인데, 부처님 말씀을 듣고 환희
   심에서 노래를 부르고 있답니다.

Guardians' Gate, 천왕문(김용사)

Four Guardians, 사천왕상(유가사)

천왕의 지물(holdings)이 사찰에 따라 조금씩 다르고 모셔진 위치도 조금씩 다르다. 대웅전을 향해, 문 입구에서 바라볼 때 왼쪽 위쪽에 북방천왕(다문천왕, pagoda)을 모셨으면 시계방향으로 동남서의 순서로 동방천왕(지국천왕, lute)과 남방천왕(증장천왕, sword)이 한 쌍이 되고, 서방천왕(광목천왕, dragon and jewel)과 북방천왕이 한 쌍이 된다. 오른쪽 위에 북방천왕을 모셨으면 동방천왕과 한 쌍을 이루고, 남방과 서방천왕이 한 쌍이 된다. 『천수경』에서 동남서북의 순으로 도량찬을 하듯이 불교에서 방향을 말할 때는 이렇게 원의 방향이다.

5. Non-Duality Gate
불이문

K: This is the last gate, the Non-Duality Gate.

F: What do you mean 'non-duality'?

K: The literal meaning is 'not-two'. For example, sacred and secular, good and evil, clean and dirty, birth and death are not two. They are not different but the same.

F: I can't understand it clearly.

K: Let me say this. Here are flowers; one is fresh and pretty, the other is faded and ugly. Then, when you talk about beauty or ugliness, it is nothing but a phenomenal aspect of a flower. In terms of essence, those are the same, not different. Likewise, mind and body, spirit and matter are not two. This has become a basic and common concept of Mahayana Buddhism. Make sense to you?

F: I think I know, but I don't think it is easy.

K: When you pass through this last gate among the three gates at temples, you have to get away from that kind of dualistic view of things. So, some temples have this gate named Liberation Gate (해탈문), which means transcending all duality and relativity.

Non-Duality Gate, 불이문(범어사)

K: 이제 마지막 문인 불이문입니다.

F: 불이不二란 무슨 뜻이죠?

K: 문자적으로는 둘이 아니라는 뜻인데 성속, 선악, 미추, 생사가 둘
   이 아니고 하나라는 뜻입니다.

F: 이해가 잘 안 되는군요.

K: 이렇게 설명해볼까요. 예를 들어 여기 싱싱하고 아름다운 꽃과
   시들어 보기 흉한 꽃이 있다고 합시다. 아름답다거나 보기 싫다
   고 하는 것은 현상일 뿐이지 본질적인 측면에서는 같은 꽃이라
   는 것이지요. 그러니까 몸과 마음, 정신과 물질 이런 것이 둘이
   아니란 거죠. 대승불교의 기본 개념이죠. 이해가 됩니까?

F: 네, 알 것도 같지만 쉽지는 않네요.

K: 산문의 마지막 문인 이 문을 지났을 때의 마음가짐은 이와 같은 이분법적인 생각에서 벗어나 있어야 한다는 것이죠. 그러니까 어떤 절에는 해탈문이라고 써 있어요. 이분법적인 관계성에서 벗어나라는 거죠.

이분법적인 사고(dualistic view of things)에 젖어서 현상만 보는 일에 익숙한 외국인들이 존재를 본질적인 측면으로 설명하는 '불이不二'를 이해하기란 쉽지 않을 것이다. 본질적으로 모든 중생은 불성(buddha-nature)을 갖추고 있어서 부처와 중생이 다르지 않다는 부처님의 가르침이 '신 중심적(god centric)'인 사고에 젖은 사람들한테는 어려운 얘기다. 불이와 함께 어려운 불교용어 중 하나인 승의제와 세속제는 각각 Absolute (Essential) Truth, Conventional Truth로 쓴다.

6. Feng-shui: Geomancy
풍수지리

Literally Feng means wind and shui means water. It is a kind of prophetic theory that energies of the earth and landscape get connected to the good or bad luck of the state and individual at present and in the future. Therefore, it is very influential and serious from the royal to the ordinary to search and choose a good site for graves, residences, palaces and even cities. This theory was introduced to Korea from China at the time of the late Silla Dynasty by Venerable Doseon.

The ideal site is considered having a mountain behind on the north, lower hills left and right, and sloped to the south. Also, there should be a river nearby that would purify the site. The capital city, Seoul, was chosen by the founding king of the Joseon Dynasty following this theory.

This theory could explain one of the reasons why the large Korean Temples are located in the deep mountains.

풍은 바람을, 수는 물을 뜻한다. 땅이나 산의 모양이 현재나 미래의 개인 혹은 국가의 길흉화복과 연결되어 있다고 보는 일종의 예언적 이론을 말한다. 왕실에서 국가의 도읍지, 궁궐의 위치, 능침 선정뿐 아니라 일반 백성들도 집터와 음택 선정에 이르기까지 그

영향력이 대단했다. 풍수지리설은 신라 말 도선 스님에 의해 중국에서 도입되었다.

이상적인 터로 배산임수를 꼽는데, 이는 뒤로(북)는 산이 있고 좌우에 뒷산보다 낮은 산이 있으며, 그 지세를 정화시키는 (강)물이 반드시 근처에 있는 곳이다. 이러한 곳의 예로 서울을 들 수 있는데, 이는 조선왕조를 건국한 태조가 선정한 곳이다.

이는 한국의 많은 큰 사찰들이 왜 산속 깊은 곳에 있는지를 설명하는 한 이유가 될 수 있다.

Part 3

Inside the Compound

1. Four Instruments (Objects) 1
사물 1

K: Here we are in the bell pavilion. There are four instruments: a Dharma drum, Brahma bell, wooden fish, and gong.

F: What are these for?

K: Let me try to give you a mental picture before I go further. It is predawn, around 3 or 4 o'clock in the morning, under a starry sky. Stillness and silence surround. Then, there comes slow and little drum sounds growing louder and louder, eventually moving your heart.

F: Wow! It must be amazing! Is it for entertainment?

K: Not really. More than that. Actually, in the morning, the temple wakes up by the sound of wooden clacker being struck by a monk as he walks slowly around the temple compounds chanting. While other monks gather in the Main Buddha Hall for the morning service, the sounds of these four objects ring out one after the other, to call up the four beings and pray for them.

K: 여기는 범종각입니다.

법고, 범종, 목어, 운판의 사물四物이 있지요.

F: 이것들은 뭐에 쓰는 겁니까?

Bell pavilion, 범종각(개심사)

K: 계속 설명하기 전에 머릿속에 이런 것을 한번 그려보세요. '새벽 3, 4시경에 하늘엔 아직 별이 총총하고 주위는 고요한데 어디선가 북소리가 들려오는 겁니다. 작고 느린 소리로 시작해서 점점 커지면서 결국 당신의 가슴을 치는 강력한 북소리가 되지요.'

F: 와! 굉장하겠네요. 일종의 오락인가요?

K: 아니지요. 그보다 더 깊은 뜻이지요. 실상 절의 하루는 도량석으로 시작됩니다. 스님이 목탁을 치면서 절 경내를 천천히 돌며 목탁 치고 염불하면서 모든 사물事物을 깨우지요. 스님들이 아침예불을 드리러 법당으로 모이는 동안 여기 사물四物 소리는 계속 이어집니다. 이것은 네 종류의 중생들을 깨우며 그들을 위해 기도드리는 소리입니다

외국인들이 절 경내에서 제일 흥미있어 하는 부분이 범종각이다. 시간이 허락하는 여행객이라면 절에서 하룻밤 자면서 아침 도량석(morning waking-up ceremony)의 목탁 소리와 사물 치는 소리를 듣는 것만으로도 한국은 분명 잊지 못할 여행지가 될 것이다.

범종각은 bell pavilion, 사물은 four objects, 목탁은 wooden clacker/striker, 죽비는 bamboo striker/clapper/stick, 요령은 buddhist hand bell, 풍경은 wind bell.

〈종송게〉

Upon hearing the sound of the bell

Defilements are eradicted,

Wisdom grows, Bodhi arises,

Leaving behind hell

Transcend three realms of samsara

Abandoning the triple world

I vow to achieve Buddhahood and save all beings.

이 종소리를 들으며 온갖 번뇌 끊어내고

청정지혜 늘어나고, 보리심 일으켜서

지옥세계 벗어나서 삼계를 떠나

깨달음 이루어 중생구제하여지이다.

(聞鐘聲 煩惱斷 /智慧長 菩提生/離地獄 出三界/願成佛 度衆生)

2. Four Instruments 2 / Three poisons
사물 2 / 삼독

F: What do you mean by praying for four other beings?

K: The Dharma drum, made of animal skin, calls the four-legged animals, the bell calls beings in hell, the wooden fish for water-borne beings, and the gong for beings of the air. We pray like this, "May all beings who hear these sounds sever their roots to the three poisons and grow their wisdom for a better next life."

F: If I do not stay and sleep at temples, I may not have chances to hear these sounds?

K: Fortunately, you have another chance. In the evening ceremony they do a similar thing. Please don't miss it.

F: By the way, what are the three poisons?

K: They are greed or craving, anger or hatred, and delusion or ignorance. They are the cause of sufferings in Buddhism. So we are concerned with removing of these poisons by cleansing the mind rather than repenting the so-called 'original sin' which is emphasized in Christianity. If you are freed from three poisons, you will be happy. Which is the toughest to control among these three poisons for you?

Wooden fish, 목어

Dharma drum and Brahma bell, 법고와 범종

F: 네 종류의 중생들을 위해서 기도하는 것이 무슨 뜻이죠?

K: 네, 북은 네 발 달린 동물을 위해서, 종은 지옥 중생을 위해서, 목
어는 수중 동물을 위해서, 운판은 날아다니는 중생을 위해서 친
답니다. 이 소리를 듣고 이들 중생들이 삼독에서 벗어나 지혜가

증장되어 보다 나은 다음 생이 되기를 기도하는 것이죠.

F: 절에서 묵지 않으면 이것을 듣기 힘들겠네요.

K: 아니죠. 저녁예불 전에도 똑같이 하니까 들을 수 있어요. 놓치지 말고 들어봐요.

F: 그런데 삼독三毒은 무엇을 말하는 거죠?

K: 그건 탐진치貪瞋癡를 말하는데, 불교에서는 고통의 원인이 여기 있다고 보지요. 그래서 기독교에서 소위 말하는 원죄를 회개해야 한다는 생각보다는 마음을 닦아서 이 삼독을 제거하는 것에 관심이 있는 것이죠. 삼독에서 벗어날 수만 있다면 행복해지는 거지요. 당신은 이 셋 중에서 무엇이 제일 조절하기 힘들어요?

사물四物에 대해 대부분의 불교서적이 대승불교적인 입장에서 위와 같은 설명을 하고 있다. 그런 점을 외국인들이 흥미있어 한다. 그러나 대승불교가 인간 중심의 종교이고, 특히 마음을 강조한다는 점을 생각할 때, 북은 동물 같은 탐욕을, 목어는 게으름(목탁의 유래 설화)을, 종은 어리석음을, 운판은 현실과 동떨어진 이상만을 추구하는 태도 등, 마음에 대한 경계를 위해 사물을 치고 기도한다는 해석이 더 어울리지 않을까 하는 생각이다.

3. Korean Brahma Bell
한국의 범종

In old days, a Brahma bell was an essential in the daily temple life to announce the timetable and regulate the mass of monks and people living in the village near temple. Sometimes the bell was struck to inform people of an emergency like forest fire, invasion of enemies, or the death of a great monk.

There is some difference between Korean Brahma bells and those of China and Japan, though the shape is somewhat similar, let alone western bells.

1) A Korean Brahma bell does not have a clapper inside, and its mouth is not broader than body. The body line falls almost the same width from the body to the brim, tapered very slightly.

2) To make a sound, a Korean bell is struck on the points on the outside of the bell marked with lotus petals in a circle at the lower part (당좌), on either side. When striking it, we use a long wooden log which is suspended from the ceiling.

3) On top of the bell are an intricately carved roaring dragon (용뉴) and a hollow sound tube(음통). The dragon is a loop used to suspend the bell from the ceiling. The hollow sound tube is connected to the body to boost the sound wave clear, far

and wide. This tube is seen only on Korean bells.

4) A Korean bell has 9 knobs (유두) set in three rows of three in the 4 square panels at the upper part of the body. These are found commonly both on Chinese and Japanese bell as well.

5) On both sides of the bell body are engraved fabulous heavenly beings playing musical instruments. There seems to be heavenly music coming from them.

6) The bell's brim is decorated with a bands of Chinese grass motifs or Arabesque motifs (당초문 혹은 보상화문).

7) A depression in the ground almost the same width of the bell mouth just below the bell is another unique feature to make the sound resonate long, far, and wide.

8) A Korean bell should not hang high up near the ceiling or in the steeple; it is placed near the ground to be easy to hit and resonate the sound.

옛날에는 절의 범종은 스님들은 물론이고 절 아래 동네 사람들에게도 일정(시간)을 알리는 역할을 했다. 그뿐 아니라 산불이나 외침, 또는 큰스님의 입적 등 위급함을 알릴 때도 종을 쳐서 알렸다.

우리의 범종은 서양종과는 말할 것도 없고 중국이나 일본 종과도 다른 특징들이 있어서 학계에서도 한국 종을 따로 분류하고 있다고 한다.

1) 서양 종은 나팔꽃 모양으로 종입구(종구)가 벌어져 있지만 범종은 눈에 띄지 않을 정도로 조금씩 좁아지지만 몸통과 거의 같은 폭의 선으로 떨어지는 우아한 형태이고, 서양 종은 종 안쪽에 종추

Sacred Bell of Great King Seongdeok, 성덕대왕신종

roaring dragon and sound tube,
범종 상부 용뉴와 음통

가 있어 그것을 움직여 땡강땡강 소리를 내지만

　2) 우리 범종은 밖에서 몸통의 아래 부분에 있는 당좌(둥근 연꽃 문양)를 쳐서 소리를 낸다. 이때 치는 굵고 둥근 나무통은 줄로 천장에 연결되어 있다.

　3) 특히 천장을 향한 종 윗 표면에는 종을 매다는 고리 역할 부분인 용뉴와 음통이 있다. 용모양의 용뉴는 '포뢰'의 전설에서 온 울부짖는 용의 모습을 사실적으로 묘사하여 아름답다. 음통 또한 다른 나라 종에서는 찾아 볼 수 없는 것으로 종 내부에서 생긴 잡음을 흡수하여 아름다운 소리를 내게 한다고 한다.

　4) 한국 종 상단 부분에는 사방으로 네모꼴 안에 세줄의 유두가 배치되어 총 36개의 유두가 있는데 이는 중국 종과 일본 종에서도 보인다.

5) 종신鐘身 양쪽에는 주악비천상이나 공양상 등으로 부조하여 천상의 음악이 들리는 듯하다.

6) 종구鐘口 바로 위를 두르고 있는 문양 띠는 당초문이나 보상화 무늬이다.

7) 종 바로 밑의 땅을 종 넓이만큼 얕게 패어서 맥놀이를 오래 가게 만드는 것도 특징이다.

8) 그러므로 범종은 교회 종처럼 종탑에 높이 매달아 놓으면 안 된다. 종구가 지표면 가까이 있어 종소리를 오래 은은하게 울리게 하며, 스님이 타종할 때 힘차게 때릴 수 있다. 〔연전에 스리랑카의 절을 방문했을 때 (아마도 우리가 기증했을텐데) 우리의 범종을 천장 높이 달아 놓은 것을 보고 놀란 적이 있다.〕

올해 초(2020년) 인사동의 한 갤러리에서 강우방 교수의 "조형 언어를 말하다" 전에서 우리가 당초문이나 보상화문으로 알고 있는 문양을 강 교수님 특유의 '영기 화생'으로 해석하면서 고구려 벽화에서부터 일본, 그리스, 로마, 파리 노트르담 성당 등의 문양을 하나로 꿰뚫는 해석이 퍽 흥미로웠다. 이는 오래 전 인도 델리 국립박물관에 갔을 때 당초 문양이 우리 절에서 보았던 문양과 너무 똑같아서 놀랐던 기억을 떠올리면서 강 교수님의 영기문靈氣紋 해석이 새롭고 신선했다.

4. Cloud-shaped Gong *(Woonpan)*

운판

When it comes to the word 'cloud', two metaphors occurred to me; one is familiar to buddhists, the other is known to many common Koreans.

The Jogye Order of Korean Buddhism keeps the 3-month-retreat tradition very strictly in summer and winter. In that period, meditating monks can not leave the temple, and they devote themselves only to *hwadu* meditation for more than fourteen hours everyday, and especially for 7-day-strenuous practice without sleeping. (The *hwadu* is an essential subject that generates spiritual inquiry.) When it is over, another 3-month-free-period awaits monks. During this free season, monks wander like a floating cloud and running water from temple to temple in the country side, and stay as long as they want, meeting family and friends or soliciting instructions from another Masters. This is one of the benefits of the Korean monastery life. We call this 'pilgrimage like clouds and water (雲水行脚).'

Another metaphor, a kind of old cliche for the young, is "to harbour a blue cloud (青雲) in your heart" which means to have a great ambition for social or political success. Interestingly, the color of the highest cloud is mostly white, and it can be blue depending on how much deep it reflects and absorbs the sun's rays. Thus, a cloud is praised as a symbol of freedom or loftiness.

Originally the gong hung at the kitchen in temples to help prevent fires because of the motif of the cloud which contains rain, and it was struck to announce mealtime when the food were ready. In this sense, the cloud of the gong was rather practical than symbolic. Now, usually being placed behind the large Dharma Bell in the Bell Pavilion, its beauty gets hardly noticed. Usually two beautiful flying, dancing celestial maidens are carved on the copper or iron plate with sun and moon or "Ohm mani pad me Hum" in Chinese characters.

As one of four ritual instruments, the gong is struck at morning and evening chanting regularly, following the drum and wooden fish. It is said that the cloud-shaped gong is sounded for the creatures of the air wishing attain the Buddha Way together with all creatures in the universe.

I'd like to pray further like this:
Hearing the sound of the cloud-shaped gong,
May the mind be free as a cloud, without attachment,
May the aspiration to Enlightenment be as lofty as a cloud.
(This was released in the English Buddhist magazine "Buddha Link" in 2006.)

구름이란 말을 생각하면 두 가지 비유가 떠오르는데, 하나는 불자들한테 익숙한 말이고, 다른 하나는 우리나라 일반인 누구나한테

Cloud-shaped Gong (*Woonpan*), 운판

나 익숙한 말이다.

조계종은 여름 겨울 각 3개월간의 안거를 철저히 지키고 있다. 안거 기간에는 선방 수좌들은 산문 밖을 나가지 않고 하루 14시간 이상을 오직 화두참구만을 한다. 특히 용맹정진 7일간은 잠을 자지 않고 계속 정진한다. (화두란 계속 의정을 일으키게 하는 주제어이다.) 안거가 끝나면 3개월의 산철이 있다. 이 산철 동안에 스님들은 흘러가는 구름처럼 여행하면서 가족, 친지들을 만나거나, 가고 싶은 다른 사찰의 큰스승을 찾아 지도를 받을 수 있다. 이는 우리 스님 생활의 장점이라 할 수 있다. 이러한 행위를 "운수행각"이라 일컫는다.

다른 비유 하나는 "청운의 뜻을 품어라" 하는 오래된 어구 중에 있는 '운'자이다. 재미있는 점이 구름의 최상층은 대개 흰색을 띠는데 햇볕을 얼마나 많이 흡수하여 반사하는가에 따라 푸른빛을 띠기도 한다고 한다. 이렇듯이 구름은 자유와 높은 기상을 표현한다.

운판의 구름 형상 때문에 (구름이 비를 머금고 있으므로) 원래는 화재 방지용으로 사찰 후원(부엌)에 걸어두었고 공양이 준비되면 공양시간을 알리기 위해 치는 용도로 쓰였지만, 현재는 범종각의 법고 뒤에 걸려 있는데 그 아름다움에 소홀한 편이다. 운판은 구름 형태의 철이나 동판 모양에 해와 달이 좌우에 있고 춤추는 천인天人 둘이 그려져 있다. 때로는 '옴마니반메훔'의 글자를 새겨 넣기도 한다.

아침저녁 예불 시간에 법고와 목어를 치고 난 뒤에 하늘에 날아다니는 중생의 해탈을 염원하면서 운판을 치는데, 여기에 붙여서 이렇게 기도하고 싶다.

깨달음을 향한 이 서원
저 높은 하늘 구름처럼
어디에도 얽매이지 않고 자유로워 지이다.

5. Wooden Clacker *(Moktak)*

목탁

It is 3 or 4 o'clock, whether it is a starry, rainy or snowy night, that the rhythmic beat of a Wooden Clacker (*Moktak*) shatters the predawn silence and stillness everyday in a temple. A monk walks around every corner of the temple, striking a wooden clacker chanting (usually reciting the Thousand Hands Sutra) and wakes up all the monks and beings still asleep. We call this Dohryangsuk; wake-up chant. The sound of a wooden clacker opens a day!

A very new beginner buddhist or a foreigner who attends the regular service in the Main Hall may feel strange to see and follow other participants who rise from their seated positions and bow or chant, even though there was no announcements or notices at all. The key is the beat of wooden clacker, which has all the attendees of the Hall rise and lead them to bow and chant. According to a long or short beat, all participants can discern when to rise or to bow, and how to recite, slowly or quickly.

Thus, a wooden clacker is always used in all the buddhists services or rituals in Korean Buddhism. It has transformed from the wooden fish which is usually hanging in the Bell Pavilion. It has gradually been rounded from a fish shape to make it easier to hold and play. However, how differently it has changed between Korean and Chinese temples, though its use is almost the same! While ours is rather small and portable, the Chinese one is far bigger than ours, placed on a certain level of a dais, unmoved, to be struck well. In Buddhism, the fish symbolizes constant effort, because a fish does not close its eyes even while asleep.

There is a very interesting legend behind the moktak.

A long, long time ago, a great old monk lived in a temple with many young disciples. Among these young monks was one who was lazy and did not practice hard and missed the mundane life. Finally, he got ill and died young.

One day, the old monk was crossing the river by the temple on a boat. Very strangely, a big tree was moving in the river following his boat. When he watched carefully, he saw it was a very peculiar fish with a tree on his back. The monk immediately entered samadhi (deep meditation) and reviewed the fish's previous lives, only to find it was his disciple who had died and who was now receiving retribution for his bad conducts as a monk; he was reborn as a fish with a tree growing out of his back and it caused him to suffer a lot.

The great monk felt pity on him and gave a grand ritual for his happy rebirth for his next life, upon arriving at his temple.

That night the old monk dreamed. His former disciple appeared to him in the dream, and deeply appreciated his kindness, asking him to cut the tree from the fish's back and to carve a fish-shaped wooden percussion instrument to be struck before the Buddha in the temple. He told the old monk that the sound of this instrument would inspire people to strive hard in their practices. The great monk followed the wishes of his disciple, and this is how the wooden clacker came about.

How about you buying one small moktak and striking it in order to check and admonish yourself when you are drifting and sinking in the ocean of indifference or laziness?

(This was released in the English Buddhist magazine "Buddha Link" in 2006.)

절집의 하루는 새벽 3시나 4시에 새벽 정적을 깨는 목탁소리로 시작된다. 이는 비가 오나 눈이 오나 사시사철 거르는 일이 없다. 스님 한 분이 목탁을 치며 천수경을 독송하면서 절 경내 구석구석을 돌며 아직 잠이 덜 깬 스님들과 일체 중생을 깨운다. 이를 도량석이라 한다. 목탁소리로 하루를 여는 것이다.

법회에 처음 참석하는 초심불자나 외국 관광객은 아무런 알림소리도 없는데 불자들 모두가 일사불란하게 일어나 절하고 독송하는 것을 보고 의아해 하기도 한다. 목탁이 그 역할을 하는 것인데, 목탁소리의 고저장단이 알림소리가 되는 것이다.

이처럼 목탁은 한국 절의 예불이나 법회에서 없어서는 안 되는 도구이다. 목탁은 범종루에 걸려 있는 사물 중의 목어를 손에 들고 칠 수 있도록 둥근 모양으로 바꾼 것이다. 같은 역할을 하는 목탁인데도 한국과 중국의 목탁의 변화는 재미있다. 우리 목탁이 작고 휴대하기 좋게 진화된 반면에 중국 목탁은 모습은 둥글지만 크기는 엄청 커서 높은 대위에 고정시켜 올려놓고 칠 수밖에 없는 모양이

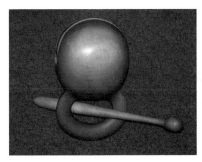

Wooden Clacker (*Moktak*), 목탁   Chinese Moktak, 중국의 목탁
(서울 불광산사)

다. 불교에서 물고기는 정진을 상징한다. 물고기는 자면서도 눈을 감지 않기 때문이다.

수행과 관련하여 목탁에 관한 재미있는 얘기가 전해지고 있다.

옛날에 큰스님 밑에서 수행하는 젊은 수행자가 있었다. 이 젊은 이는 수행에 관심이 별로 없었고 세속을 그리워하다 병이 들어 그만 일찍 죽고 말았다. 어느 날 큰스님이 배를 타고 강을 건너는데 등에 큰 나무가 박힌 물고기 한 마리가 계속 따라왔다. 스님이 이상히 여기고 선정에 들어 그 물고기의 전생을 살펴보았더니 그 물고기는 바로 죽은 제자였다. 생전에 수행을 게을리한 과보를 그런 모습으로 받은 것이었다. 스님은 그 제자를 불쌍히 여겨 절에 오자마자 천도재를 크게 지내주었다.

그날 밤 꿈에 그 제자가 나타나서 감사를 드리며, 등에서 자란 나무를 베어서 법회 때마다 두드리게 해서 자기처럼 게으른 수행자를 경책해 달라고 부탁을 했다고 한다.

우리도 작은 목탁 하나 사서 마음이 산란하고 방일해질 때마다 목탁을 쳐서 스스로를 경책해 봄이 어떨까?

6. Pagoda and Sarira

탑과 사리

K: When we Koreans say the word 'tap', it denotes 'pagoda' or 'stupa' in the temple.

F: 'Tap' sounds like a tower in English.

K: It is totally different from the bell tower in the church or castle in western countries. The (bell) tower is only to house a ringing bell, isn't it? Pagoda comes from 'stupa' in Sanskrit. I have to mention sarira to explain more. Do you know what sarira is, by any chance?

F: As far as I know, it is bead-like relics left after cremation of a body.

K: You're right. According to records, 84,000 relics were produced from the historical Buddha Sakyamuni. They were distributed to eight countries and deposited in pagodas to be worshipped.

F: That's why many people bow to pagodas and walk around them.

K: Exactly. In the earliest era, only the historical Buddha's relics were enshrined but later, Sutras, his teachings, were placed inside the stupa, and became a central object of Buddhist worship.

K: 한국 사람들이 탑이라고 말할 때 그건 절에 있는 탑을 말하는 거예요.

F: 탑이라는 발음이 영어의 타워와 비슷하네요.

K: 그렇게 들리기도 하지만 교회나 성안에 있는 종탑과는 전혀 다른 겁니다. 종탑은 그저 종을 치기 위해 높이 종을 보관하는 곳이지요. 파고다는 범어의 스투파에서 유래한 것이거든요. 탑을 설명하려면 사리를 얘기해야겠어요. 혹시 '사리'에 관해 알아요?

F: 화장한 뒤에 나오는 구슬같이 생긴 유물로 알고 있는데요.

K: 잘 알고 있네요. 기록에 따르면 부처님한테서 84,000개의 사리가 나왔는데 여덟 나라에 분배되어서 탑 안에 봉안되었어요.

F: 그래서 사람들이 탑을 향해 절하고 탑돌이를 하는군요.

Three-story Stone Pagoda
at Gameunsa Temple Site,
감은사지 삼층석탑

K: 네, 맞아요. 초기에는 탑에 부처님의 진신사리만 모셨지만 나중
  에는 경을 봉안하기도 해서 예배의 대상이 된 거죠.

사리舍利는 산스크리트의 '사리라'의 음역이니까 한자에 아무런 뜻이
없다. 그렇다고 외국인들에게 '사리라'라고 말하면 그게 뭐냐고 되묻는
다. relic이라고 말해주면 이해를 한다.
탑돌이를 번역할 때 주로 walking around a stupa라고 하는데 경
전에서 우요삼잡右繞三匝이라고 나오고 circumambulated the
Buddha three times to the right라고 번역하니까 어렵더라도
circumambulation을 썼으면 한다.

7. Counting the Tiers

탑의 층수

Most pagodas seen today in Korea are made of stone. However, since when Buddhism reached Korea, pagodas were built of wood. As time passed, almost two centuries after, wooden pagodas were replaced with stones, since many good quality stones, like granite were available. There was also the development of techniques dealing them, yet they are patterned after a wooden structure. The exemplary pagoda for this is the five-tier stone pagoda on the ruin site of Jeongnimsa Temple in Buyo, whose roof stones are thin, wide and yet slightly raised at the end of the eaves, just like those made of wood. It looks great and is very artistic.

In the earliest era, pagodas were enshrined only with the historical Buddha's relics but later, Sutras were placed inside and became a central object of Buddhist worship. They became adorned with various motifs such as Buddhas, Bodhisattvas and the twelve Spirit Generals (12신장).

A pagoda has three parts: the base, body, and finial. When we refer to the numbers of tiers of a pagoda, only roof stones of the body part are counted. Generally, odd numbers are chosen for the numbers of tiers of pagodas. It comes from the old Oriental Cosmic Principles: Yin and Yang theory. Yin and Yang are opposite but supplementary forces to each other. Yang, odd numbers are considered to be male, noble, light, and auspicious, with 9 being the culmination of yang as counting the tiers. The theory has no direct connection with Buddhism, but was assimilated into it.

요즘 남아 있는 탑은 거의가 석탑이다. 그러나 불교가 중국을 거쳐 들어오면서 목탑 형식이 함께 들어왔다. 거의 2세기의 세월이 흐르면서 목탑은 석탑으로 대치되었는데, 이는 화강석 같은 좋은 돌이 발견되었고 그것을 다루는 기술도 함께 발달했기 때문이라고 볼 수 있다. 그러나 아직은 목탑의 흔적이 남아 있다. 이러한 과도기의 전형적인 탑 형식이 부여에 있는 정림사지의 5층 석탑이다. 판석이 돌인데도 여전히 목탑처럼 얇고 평평하면서 지붕의 처마끝

Five-story Stone Pagoda
at Jeongnimsa Temple Site,
정림사지 오층석탑

이 들리듯이 그 끝이 날렵하게 들려진 것이 미적 감각이 돋보인다.

탑 조성 초기에는 부처님의 사리를 탑에 봉안하였으나 점차 불경이 봉안되면서 예배의 대상이 되었고, 부처와 보살상, 그밖에 12지신장상 등을 조각하여 장엄하였다.

탑은 기단부, 탑신부, 상륜부의 세 부분으로 구분한다. 탑이 몇 층인지 셀 때는 탑신부만을 계산한다. 일반적으로 몇 층 탑인지는 기수로 결정한다. 이는 동양사상의 음양설에서 기원하는데 음과 양은 서로 반대되면서도 보완적인 힘을 말한다. 기수인 양수는 '9'를 정점으로 주로 남성성, 귀(貴)함, 밝음, 상서로움 등을 상징한다. 이러한 이론이 불교와는 직접적인 연관은 없으나 불교에 녹아들었다고 할 수 있다.

8. You'll see a famous pagoda there
다보탑

K: Do you have an old 10 won coin?

F: What for? Do you need it for the phone?

K: No, I want you to look at one side of it carefully. You'll see a famous pagoda there.

F: Let me see. Ah! Isn't this the one I saw at Bulguksa temple the other day?

K: Definitely! Its name is Many Treasures/Jeweled Pagoda, one of two pagodas located side by side in front of the Main Buddha Hall. The other is Sakyamuni Pagoda. They have profound meaning.

F: What is it?

K: The area symbolizes the Dharma Assembly at Vulture Peak in India. It depicts the Many Treasures Buddha (Prabhutaratna) appearing out of the earth to testify and praise Sakyamuni Buddha's preaching of the Lotus Sutra. Another noteworthy of the Sakyamuni Pagoda is the Great Dharani Sutra of Immaculate and Pure Light (무구정광 대다라니경), which was discovered during the second repairing of the Sakyamuni Pagoda in 1966. It is known as the oldest sutra printed by carved wooden blocks in the world, and its size is 6.7 centimeters wide, and 6.2 meters long in a paper scroll.

K: 우리 돈 10원 짜리 구 동전 있어요?

F: 왜 뭐에 쓰려고요? 공중전화 걸려고요?

K: 아니요. 동전의 한 면을 자세히 봐요. 거기 보면 유명한 탑이 있거든요.

F: 어디 봅시다. 아, 이거요? 지난번 불국사에서 봤던 탑 아닙니까?

K: 맞아요. 다보탑이라고 해요. 대웅전 앞에 나란히 있는 탑 두 개 중 하나지요. 다른 것은 석가탑이라고 해요. 이 두 탑에는 깊은 뜻이 있답니다.

F: 뭔데요?

K: 그 공간은 부처님이 영축산에서 설법하는 장면을 상징하고 있어요. 석가여래께서 『법화경』을 설하실 때 다보여래께서 땅에서

Many Treasures/Jeweled Pagoda,
다보탑

솟아나 석가모니 부처님의 설법을 증명하는 장면입니다. 그리고 또 하나 석가탑에서 주목할 것은 1966년 석가탑 보수공사 때 발견된『무구정광대다라니경』입니다. 이것은 세계에서 가장 오래된 목판 인쇄본인데 폭은 6.7cm지만 그 길이가 6.2m미터에 달하는 긴 두루마리 경이지요.

유명한 불국사의 다보탑과 석가탑을 얘기할 때『삼국유사』에 나오는 아사달과 아사녀의 무영탑(석가탑)에 관한 설화는 회자되어도 이것이 정작『법화경』견보탑품(The Emergence of the Treasure Tower)을 형상화한 것이라는 것을 아는 사람이, 심지어 불자들도 드문 것이 안타깝다.

9. The Emergence of the Treasure Tower (Many Jeweled Tower)

『법화경』 견보탑품 일부

At that time there was a bodhisattva-mahasattva named Great Joy in Preaching (Mahapratibhana), addressed the Buddha, saying, "O World-Honored One! For what reason has this treasure tower risen up out of the earth? And why does this voice issue from its midst?"

At that time, the Buddha said: "Great Joy in Preaching, within this jeweled stupa is the whole body of a Thus Come One. Long ago, an immeasurable thousand, ten thousand, million asamkhyas of worlds to the east, in a land called Treasure Purity, there was a Buddha named Many Treasures. When this Buddha was originally carrying out the bodhisattva way, he made a great vow, saying, 'If, after I have become a Buddha and entered extinction, in the lands in the ten directions there is any place where the Lotus Sutra is preached, then my funerary tower (stupa-shrine), in order that I may listen to the sutra, will come forth and appear in that spot to testify to the sutra by praising it, saying Excellent!'"

– from The Lotus Sutra translated by Burton Watson –

그때 대요설이라 부르는 한 보살마하살이 부처님께 아뢰었다.

"세존이시여, 무슨 인연으로 저 보배탑이 땅속에서 솟아나왔으며, 또 어떤 분이 탑 속에서 저렇게 큰 소리를 내시나이까?"

그때 부처님께서 대요설보살에게 이르시었다. "저 보배탑 속에는 여래의 몸 전체가 모셔져 있느니라. 먼 옛날 동방으로 한량없는 천만억 아승기의 수많은 세계를 지나서, 보정 세계가 있었느니라. 그 세계에 부처님께서 계셨으니, 바로 다보부처님이셨느니라. 그 부처님께서 보살도를 닦고 계실 때 큰 서원을 세우셨으니 '만약 내가 성불하고 나서 열반한 뒤 시방세계 어느 곳이든 법화경을 설하는 곳이 있다면, 나의 탑이 경을 듣기 위해 그 앞에 솟아나리라. 그리고 설법을 증명하기 위해 거룩하다고 찬탄하리라.'"

－『우리말 법화경』/ 혜조 스님 번역 －

Sakyamuni Pagoda and Many Jeweled Pagoda, 석가탑과 다보탑(불국사)

10. Apsaras: Celestial Beings
비천상

(in front of a Bramah Bell)

F: I've seen a similar picture of these flying figures hung on the wall of the living room at the guest house I stay. Oh, the actual figure is on the bell.

K: That must be from a rubbing; this bell is a replica as well. The original one, the Divine Bell of King Seong Deok of the Silla Dynasty, which is National Treasure No. 29, is preserved in Kyung-Joo National Museum now.

F: The figure seems to be holding something in hands.

K: Definitely. We call this 'offering type of apsara' (공양 비천상). It depicts kneeling apsaras offering something with both hands, very politely praying for the happy rebirth of the deceased king.

F: Then, these apsaras are found only on bells?

K: Apsaras in paintings are easily found on the ceiling, main altar, outside walls, or under the eaves of main halls. We have another amazing apsara called 'performing type of apsara (주악비천상)' on the Sangwonsa Temple bell, where two apsaras are playing a mouth organ and a vertical harp. When you see apsaras, please notice those long and narrow ribbon-like sashes floating above the head. Those streamers allow them fly in the air lightly. Could you imagine those light sashes playing a role like an engine? Whenever I look at this scene, I could hear fanciful heavenly music filling in the air even here around us as well. I want you to hear it and to sense the vibe of live and blissful fluttering movements in the wind.

(범종 앞에서)

F: 이와 비슷한 그림이 게스트 하우스 벽에 걸려 있어요. 실제는 종 표면에 있는 거군요.

K: 그건 아마도 탁본일 거예요. 이 종도 국보 29호인 성덕대왕신종의 복제품인데요, 진짜는 경주 박물관에 있지요.

F: 뭔가를 손에 들고 있군요.

K: 맞아요. 이건 공양비천상이라고 해요. 돌아가신 왕의 천도를 빌며 공양을 올리는 비천상인데, 꿇어앉아서 두 손으로 공양물을 공손하게 올리는 모습이지요.

F: 그럼 이런 비천상은 종에만 있어요?

K: 그림으로는 대웅전의 천장, 상단, 외벽이나 처마 밑에서도 볼 수 있어요. 이것 말고도 주악비천상이 있어요. 두 비천이 공후와 생황을 연주하고 있지요. 상원사 범종에서 볼 수 있어요. 비천상을 볼 때 특히 머리 위로 휘날리는 리본 같은 긴 띠를 눈여겨보세요. 저 긴 리본으로 공중을 마음대로 날아다니는 겁니다. 저 가벼운 리본이 엔진 같은 역할을 한다는 것이 상상이 돼요? 이걸 볼 때마다 천상의 음악소리가 여기까지 들리는 것 같아요. 당신도 그

Offering type Apsara, 성덕대왕신종의 공양비천상

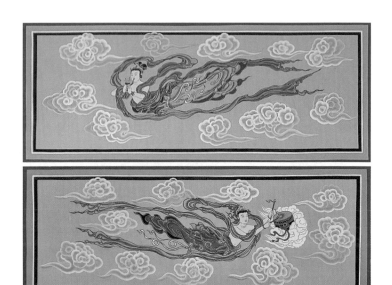

Apsara, 비천상

소리와 함께 비천인들의 생동감 넘치고 행복하게 움직이는 분위
기를 느꼈으면 해요.

절에서 제일 좋아하는 부분이 비천상이다. 조계사 시절, 어느 외국 여
자 관광객이 비천상 머리 위쪽에 둘린 리본을 가리키면서 이것이 무엇
이냐고 물었다. 천의天衣의 일부라고 말했더니 그녀의 눈빛이 '너 모르
는구나'라고 말하고 있었다. 안내를 마치고 찾아보니 우리말로는 표대
혹은 박대라고 하며, 그것으로 하늘을 날아다닌다는 것을 알았다. 수
원 용주사 범종에도 공양비천상이 있다.

11. Dragon and Lion Images
불교에서의 용과 사자

K: Have you noticed any animal images in Korean Temples that are interesting or strange to you?

F: Yes, I have seen some. Lions which support a heavy pagoda on their heads, and many dragon decorations inside and outside of the Main Hall.

K: You have a keen eye. Lions have been accepted as the protectors of the Buddha and the Dharma.

F: That's easy to understand, since the lion is the king of animals.

K: That's it. Therefore, we have many related symbolic words like 'lion's roar (사자후)' that describes Buddha's teachings and 'lion's seat (사자좌)', which refers to Buddha's seat to show Buddha's solemnity.

F: Then, how about dragons? As you know, dragons are evil things to be repelled or have a fire image to westerners.

K: Exactly. It reminds me of the tales of Sleeping Beauty. The prince fought with the terrific dragon to save the princess. However, in Buddhism a dragon is one of eight protectors of supernatural beings (8부신중) that keep away evil spirits.

F: Does it come from a kind of Korean's own folklore?

K: No, originally the 'nagas and nagins' (serpents) were

Dragon, 용

worshipped as spirits of rivers and fountains in India. These snake images transformed in favor of powerful dragon appearance. When Buddhism spread into Korea through China, it mixed with Korean folklore and snake images turned into dragon. So the wisdom dragon ship (반야용선), which leads sentient beings to the Pure Land, is depicted like a dragon. The painting is easily found outside of the Dharma Hall.

K: 한국 사찰에서 재미있거나 이상하다고 생각한 동물상 같은 거 본 적 있어요?

F: 네, 머리 위에 무거운 탑을 이고 있는 사자와 대웅전 안팎에 많이 있는 용이요.

K: 잘 보았군요. 사자는 부처님과 법을 수호하는 신중으로 받아들여져서 그래요.

F: 사자가 동물의 왕이니까 그렇게 쉽게 이해되네요.

K: 그래서 부처님의 위엄을 나타내는 여러 상징적인 말들이 있어요. 사자후 혹은 사자좌 같은 말이죠.

F: 그렇다면 용은 왜죠? 용은 서양에서는 물리쳐야 할 나쁜 상대나 불의 이미지거든요.

K: 나도 어렸을 때 읽은 동화 「잠자는 숲 속의 미녀」에서 왕자가 무서운 용과 싸우는 장면이 기억나요. 그러나 불교에서는 용은 부처님을 옹호하는 8부 신중 중의 하나지요.

F: 한국의 민속에서 나오는 건가요?

K: 아니요. 원래 인도에서 뱀을 숭배하는 사상이 있었는데, 불교가 중국을 통해 한국으로 오면서 뱀의 모습이 더 근사한 용으로 바뀌었고, 중생을 서방 정토로 인도하는 반야용선은 용의 모습으로 그려지고 있답니다. 이 그림은 법당 외벽에서 쉽게 볼 수 있어요.

Twin Lion Stone Lantern, 쌍사자 석등(법주사)

12. Floral Latticework Doors

꽃살문

To make offerings with six objects is to show reverence to the Three Jewels (Buddha, Dharma, and Sangha) and to praise them, wishing for blessings from Buddhas and Bodhisattvas. Flowers are one of the six offerings representing endurance in 6 paramitas (perfections). It is because blossoming a piece of a flower requires much of a farmer's endurance and sweat.

Today, plenty of natural fresh flowers are available regardless of the season. You can adorn the main altar with many kinds of fresh flowers as you please at any time, but in ancient times, fresh flowers were limited; only paper-made, and rarely silk-made, which were crafted were available.

Usually, the entrances on either side of the Main Buddha Hall have simple motives of belted grid (띠살) or diagonal grid (솟을 빗살) doors. However, ancestors might have come up with an idea, what if the whole facade entrances were adorned with flowers that do not fade away for good, even though they lose their colors to time. When you stand facing the amazing floral lattice door and look at them, (especially at Jeongsusa Temple on Kanghwa Island near Seoul, or Naesosa Temple in Jolla Province), it would lead you to feel as if you were offering bunches of flowers to the Buddha at the moment.

Floral Latticework patterns, 솟을 빗꽃살문양

Flowers on this latticework are diverse, including lotus, peonies, chrysanthemums, roses, and even pine trees.

육법 공양을 올리는 것은 삼보께 예경·찬탄드리면서 불보살님들의 가피를 바라는 일이다. 꽃이 6법 공양물 중에 하나가 된 것은 꽃 한송이를 피우기 위한 농부의 끈질긴 노력과 기다림의 결과물이기 때문이리라.

요즈음은 사시사철 생화가 넘쳐나서 아무 때나 마음만 먹으면 얼마든지 꽃 공양을 맘껏 올릴 수 있다. 그러나 옛날에는 생화는 귀해서 종이꽃으로 공양 올렸고, 드물게 비단으로 만든 꽃을 썼다. 물론 둘 다 품이 많이 드는 수공예였다.

법당 양쪽의 작은 출입문에는 띠살 문양이나 솟을 빗살 문양의 소박한 문을 달았다. 그러나 우리 조상들은 불전 전면을 색은 조금 바래도 시들지 않는 꽃으로 장엄하고 싶은 마음을 꽃살문으로 표현

belted grid door, 띠살문

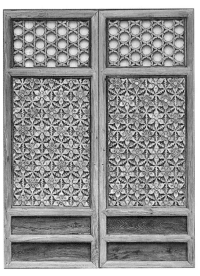

upright diagonal floral door,
솟을 빗꽃살문

diagonal grid door, 빗살문

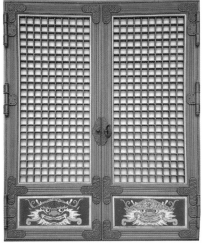

vertical and horizontal strips door, 정자문

138

했던 것 같다. 세월에 빛바래긴 했어도, 강화 정수사나 내소사 꽃살문 앞에 서면 마치 내가 한 아름의 꽃을 부처님께 공양하는 듯한 생각이 들기도 한다.

꽃살문 문양은 연꽃을 비롯해서 모란, 국화, 장미, 소나무 등 다채롭다.

꽃살문 앞에 서서 이것이 '솟을 꽃살문'인지 '솟을 빗꽃살문'인지 따지는 불자는 아마도 거의 없을 것이다. 외국인들한테도 그런 설명은 필요 없을 것이다. 그 아름다움의 감동이 첫눈에 그대로 전해지기 때문이다. 혹 번역이 필요한 사람에게 참고가 될까 해서 자료를 올린다.

띠살문 belted grid door, 빗살문 diagonal grid door, 솟을 빗살문 upright diagonal grid door, 솟을 빗꽃살문 upright diagonal floral design (pattern) door, 정자문 vertical and horizontal strips pattern door, 아자문 亞 character door

13. Swastika and Three Dots
만卍자와 원이삼점

F: I was surprised to see many swastikas in Korean temples. I'm sure you know why. Tell me.

K: I understand what you felt. I met some foreign tourists feeling uncomfortable to see the swastika mark on rafters or roof tiles. It is a symbol of Buddhism and temples in Korea. You might have seen thousands of these signs on Korean maps too. It tells us "Here is a temple."

F: Then, is it the same or different from Hakenkreuz?

K: Originally, it was the same, indicating good luck and virtue, just the facing direction was different. Hakenkreuz is right facing while we use both, right and left facing. It was found as a diverse decorative motif among ancient Indians, Greeks and even North American natives. The German nation had the same tradition and Hitler adopted it, I think.

F: How does it come into Buddhism?

K: There's a saying when the Buddha was born as a human, as a result of accumulated good virtues through many previous lives, he had 32 auspicious major marks and 80 minor signs. Among them, were a white hair between the eyebrows and body hairs curling to the right. This rightward motion accords with cosmic principles being considered

Three Dots in one circle and Swastika, 원이삼점과 만자

auspicious. When Buddhism came to Korea through China, it became a homophone with the Chinese word for 'ten thousand,' expressing countless virtues are gathered. We call it 'mahn' in Korean, and it has been used as a major sign of temples. If you look carefully there are many modifications of this motif on the stone wall of old palaces or subway stations.

F: What is the meaning of those three dots in one circle?

K: Three dots represents many things: the three jewels (Buddha, his teachings, and Sangha), the three learnings (precepts, meditation and wisdom), and the Three Dharma Seals (impermanence, suffering, and no-self). One large circle means Dharmadathu or ultimate reality (법계). All are symbols of Buddha's teachings.

F: 한국 절에 스와스티카(卐) 표시가 많은 것 보고 놀랐어요. 왜죠?

K: 이해합니다. 관광객 중에서 더러 처마나 지붕에 있는 그 표식을 보고 불쾌해하는 걸 가끔 봅니다. 한국에서는 불교와 사찰의 상징이에요. 혹시 한국 지도를 보았는지 모르지만, 지도상에 이 표시가 수없이 많은데 그곳에 절이 있다는 표식입니다

F: 그렇다면 독일의 하켄크로이츠하고는 같은 겁니까, 다른 겁니까?

K: 원래 복덕과 길상을 표시하는 의미에서는 같지요. 도는 방향만 다른 뿐. 우리는 좌만(卍)과 우만(卐) 둘 다 쓰는데, 하켄크로이츠는 우만이지요. 게르만 족에도 이런 전통이 있었고 히틀러가 그걸 차용한 것이겠죠.

Swastikas on wall, 담장의 만자 도안

F: 불교와는 어떻게 연결이 된 거죠?

K: 다겁생의 선업의 공덕으로 부처가 사람 몸을 받았을 때 32상 80종호의 신체적 특징이 있었다고 해요. 그 가운데 두 눈썹 사이의 백호와 신체의 털이 오른쪽으로 말려 있었답니다. 이것이 우주의 원리와 맞는 것으로 생각해서 길상으로 여겼지요. 불교가 중국을 거쳐 우리나라에 들어오면서 중국어와 이음동이어 현상이 생겼고, 우리말로는 '만'으로 읽으면서 만덕의 의미로 사찰에서 쓰였습니다. 잘 보면 궁궐 담장이나 지하철 벽화에서도 변형된 만자 도안을 쉽게 볼 수 있어요.

F: 그럼 저기 원 안의 세 개 점은 뭐지요.

K: 세 개의 점은 삼보, 혹은 삼학이나 삼법인을, 큰 원은 법계를, 즉 모두 부처님의 가르침을 상징해요.

14. Cosmic Design at temples
단청

F: Wow! These bright, flashy colors make a beautiful scene, and they're painted right on the building!

K: We call this the cosmic design, *danchong* in Korean. The literal meaning is red and blue.

F: Must be because red and blue are the basic colors, although there are more.

K: You got it. The Korean basic primary colors are red, blue, yellow, white and black. Other colors are produced by mixing them properly to go well with natural surroundings to bring them into the structure. For instance, brown pillars are similar to old pine trunks, and colors under the eaves are like green pine needles. Various repeating patterns show continuity and eternity signifying good fortune. There are two purposes for these paintings. One is very practical; to protect the walls from humidity, dryness, or insects, and to cover cracked low quality lumber. The other purpose is very socio-political.

F: What do you mean by that?

K: This was used only for some special buildings such as palaces or temples. Dignifying them with this brilliant adornment is the other purpose.

Cosmic Design (*Dancheong*), 단청

F: 화폭이 아닌 건물에 이렇게 화려한 색깔이 아름답게 조화를 이루다니!

K: 이것을 우리는 단청이라고 하는데, 문자적인 뜻은 빨강과 파랑이란 뜻이죠.

F: 다른 색깔도 많지만 빨강색과 파란색이 주조를 이루기 때문인 모양이군요.

K: 맞아요. 흑백녹황청의 5색을 주조로 하여 주위 환경과 잘 어울리는 색을 만들어서 자연을 건물 안으로 끌어들인 거지요. 예를 들어서 갈색 기둥색은 늙은 소나무 줄기 색과 비슷하고, 처마색은 소나무 잎 색과 비슷한 것이에요. 다양한 무늬를 반복하면서

연속성과 영원성을 보여주고 길상을 표시하는 거지요. 단청을 하는 데는 두 가지 목적이 있어요. 아주 실리적인 면으로는 습기와 건조, 벌레들의 피해를 막고 목재의 품질이 떨어지거나 금이 간 것을 감추기 위해서지요. 다른 것은 사회, 정치적인 의미가 있어요.

F: 무슨 뜻이죠?

K: 단청은 궁이나 절 같은 특별 건물에만 썼거든요. 이렇게 화려하게 장엄함으로써 위엄을 나타내는 것이죠.

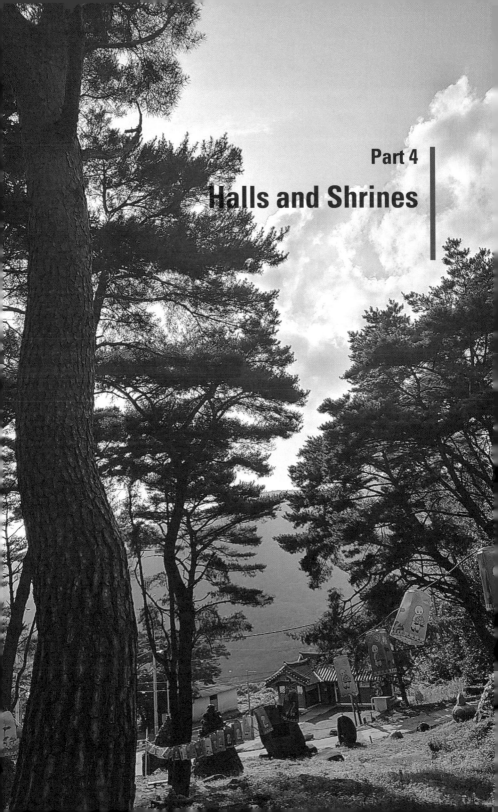

Part 4
Halls and Shrines

1. Great Hero Hall 1
대웅전 1

K: Usually, the Main Buddha Hall, *Daewoong Jeon*, is positioned in the center of the compound and is named after the Buddha enshrined inside. The name of this hall is the Great Hero Hall. Can you guess which buddha is enshrined in this hall?

F: Super easy. The Great Hero, Sakyamuni Buddha.

K: Definitely! He was born as a prince of a small kingdom in northeast India in the 5th century BCE and got enlightened in his own way, discarding his 6-year ascetic practice. He taught his truth on the road until he died at the age of 80. I'll tell you a more detailed story looking at the paintings on the outside walls of this hall. Sometimes when three

Great Hero Hall,
대웅전(수덕사)

Sakyamuni Buddha in Great Hero Hall, 대웅전 석가모니불

Buddhas are enshrined in this main hall, we call it 'Jeweled Hall of the Great Hero,' '*Daewoong Bo Jeon*' in Korean. That is Sakyamuni attended by Buddhas that are Amitabha and Bhaisajyaguru instead of bodhisattvas.

F: Is this the place lay people pray all the time?

K: Yes, all kinds of religious ceremonies and services are held here; Dharma discourses and memorial rituals are given here, as well as 3 or 4 times of daily routine chanting.

K: 법당이나 전각의 이름은 안에 모셔놓은 부처님이나 보살님의 이름을 따서 지어요. 이 법당은 대웅전이라고 해요. 그럼 여긴 어떤 부처님이 계실까요?

F: 아주 쉬운 질문이군요. 대웅이신 석가모니 부처님이지요.

K: 네, 맞았어요. 부처님은 기원전 5세기경에 인도 북동부에서 왕자로 태어나셨지요. 6년의 고행 수행을 버리고 스스로의 힘으로 성불하시고 80세에 돌아가실 때까지 길 위에서 진리를 가르치셨어요. 더 자세한 얘기는 법당 밖 벽화를 보면서 얘기하지요. 가끔 세 분의 부처님, 즉 석가모니불과 아미타불과 약사불을 같이 모셨을 때는 대웅보전이라고 불러요.

F: 그럼 이곳은 불자들이 항상 기도하는 곳이에요?

K: 모든 종교적인 행사와 불공이 베풀어지는 곳이죠. 매일 서너 차례 올리는 예불은 물론이고 법회도 하고 재(제사)를 지내기도 해요.

2. Great Hero Hall: 3 Altars
대웅전: 불단

Inside the Main Hall, there are 3 altars or platforms. The main altar is in the center toward the back wall. It includes major statues and a huge painting behind the Buddha image. The painting, *Tangwha* in Korean, matches the Buddha image in front. Usually it is the 'Dharma Assembly on Mt Gridhaguta (영산회상도)' where the Buddha delivered the Lotus Sutra. As a holy altar for the Buddhas and Bodhisattvas, this main altar is adorned with various patterns or paintings with auspicious animals or beautiful flowers.

To the left of the main altar is the Guardians' altar. This altar has only a Guardians Painting without statues, and it is composed of usually 8 to 104 guardians depending on the temples.

To the right of the main altar is the Memorial altar where the tablet or pictures of the deceased are placed for the memory of them and to use at the memorial services. The painting on the wall is 'Sweet Dew (감로도)' or 'Picture of Amitabha leading the deceased to the Pure Land (아미타내영도).'

To enter the Main Hall, laity should use the side doors on the left or right; the door in the center is reserved for monks only. Make sure to do a half bow to the Buddha entering the Main

Memorial altar, 신중단 화엄신중(석종사)

Hall or other halls or shrines.

Most wooden Korean buildings are constructed without nail, (if used, it is wooden nail) each wooden part carefully fits together perfectly with the others. Therefore it would not be so hard to dismantle the whole structure, move it from one site to another site, and reassemble it. How eco-friendly it is!

대웅전에는 불단이 셋 있다. 상단은 후면 벽을 뒤로하여 중앙에 있으며, 높은 상단에 주존불을 봉안하고 주존불 뒤 벽에는 주불과 연관된 탱화가 있다. 대체로 부처님이 영축산에서 『법화경』을 설하시는 영산회상도가 일반적이다. 상단 불단은 상서로운 동물 형상이나 아름다운 꽃그림, 조각으로 화려하게 장엄한다.

상단에서 바라볼 때 왼편에 신중단이 있다. 신중단에는 조상물 없이 신중탱화만을 봉안한다. 신중도의 신중들은 절에 따라 다르지만 적게는 8위에서 많게는 104위의 신중이 그려져 있다.

영단은 오른편에 있는데 제단 위에는 돌아가신 분의 위패와 영정을 모셔 놓는다. 영단 탱화는 감로도나 아미타내영도를 모신다.

일반 신도들은 법당 오른쪽이나 왼쪽의 문으로 드나들고 정면의 가운데 문(어간)은 스님들만 이용한다. 대웅전이나 다른 전각 출입 시에 불상을 향해 합장 반배하는 것도 잊지 말아야 한다.

대부분의 사찰 건물은 목재 건물로 못을 사용하지 않고 각 부분의 목재를 서로 완전하게 끼워 맞추는 방식이다. 그렇기 때문에 해체와 재조립이 쉬워서 다른 장소로 옮겨도 원형을 유지할 수 있는 장점이 있다. 얼마나 자연친화적인가!

3. Jeweled Palace of Tranquil Extinction
적멸보궁

F: I found a Main Buddha Hall that has no Buddha image on the altar.

K: Then, there must be a large window in the hall, and you see a stupa through the window. The stupa contains the actual relics of the historical Buddha. It represents the Buddha itself, and there is no need for placing a statue. This hall is considered superior to other halls and we call it 'Jeweled Palace of Tranquil Extinction,' meaning Sublime Treasure House.

F: What do you mean by 'tranquil extinction?'

K: It is a calm and unmoving state of mind, transcending all defilements and illusion. They say it's a state of full freedom where no birth and death exists.

F: Do you have more temples like this?

K: Yes, we have 5 more Jeweled Palace across the country.

F: 불단에 부처상이 없는 법당을 봤어요.

K: 그곳엔 틀림없이 큰 창이 있었을 겁니다. 창 너머에는 탑이 보였을 거구요. 그 탑 안에는 역사적인 부처님의 사리가 있어서 부처님을 상징하고 있으니까 상을 따로 둘 필요가 없어요. 우리는 이

Jeweled Palace of Tranquil Extinction, 적멸보궁(통도사)

법당을 다른 법당보다 더 소중하게 생각해서 "적멸보궁"이라 불러요.

F: 적멸이란 뭘 말하는 건가요?

K: 번뇌 망상을 초월하여 어떤 경계에도 끄달리지 않고 더 이상 생사가 없는 완전한 해탈 상태를 말해요.

F: 그럼 이런 법당이 또 있나요.

K: 네, 전국에 다섯 군데가 있어요.

대웅보전이나 적멸보궁에서 '보'를 영어로 번역할 때 jewel/treasure를 많이 쓴다. 대웅보전은 Jeweled Hall of the Great Hero이 된다. 보

통 세 분의 부처님, 즉 아미타불, 석가모니불, 약사여래불 등의 삼불이
나 혹은 청정법신, 원만보신, 천백억화신의 삼신불(Threefold body of a
Buddha that are Dharmakaya (Law body), Sambhogakaya (Reward body),
and Nirmanakaya (Transformational body)을 모셨을 때 보전이라 하는
데, 현판에는 대웅보전이라 하고 석가모니 부처님 한 분만을 모신 곳도
흔히 볼 수 있다. 옛날(건축 당시)에는 세 분을 모셨던 흔적일 수 있다.

Triads: 삼존불(아미타불·석가모니불·약사여래불)(석종사)

4. Supreme Bliss Hall/ Infinite Life Hall/ Infinite Light Hall 1
극락전/무량수전/무량광전 1

F: Though this hall seems to be located in the center of this temple, the name of the hall is not the Great Hero Hall.

K: This hall is dedicated to the Amitabha Buddha. He governs the western paradise or pure land, land of no suffering. We call this hall the Supreme Bliss Hall, or also the Infinite Life Hall or the Infinite Light Hall.

F: Why the western quarter? Then is there no paradise in the east?

K: I think it is because India is very hot in the daytime, so people might feel relief when the sun goes down in the western sky. The sunrise direction, east is the pure land of Lapis Lazuli Light, Bhaisajyaguru, Healing Buddha's land, representing the birth of new life.
There lived Dharmakara Bhiksu a Bodhisattva of vows, had taken 48 great vows before getting Enlightened. Among them, if sentient beings call on Amitabha's name only 10 times wholeheartedly even near death, they could come to this pure land, the best place to be reborn.

F: Then it sounds different from the Sakyamuni Buddha's teaching "Rely upon yourself and make my teachings your

Infinite Life Hall, 무량수전(홍천사)

light."

K: Well, this is a skillful means to attain liberation depending on Faith in Other Power, which is the blessing of Buddhas and Bodhisattvas.

F: 이 전각은 사찰의 중심에 있는데도 대웅전이라 쓰여 있지 않군요.

K: 아미타 부처님을 모신 전각이죠. 서방정토에 계신 부처님이에요. 무량수전이나 무량광전이라고도 불러요.

F: 서방에요? 그럼 동방에는 없나요?

K: 아마 인도가 더운 나라니까, 서쪽으로 해가 지면 편안함을 느끼

게 되어 서쪽을 택한 거겠지요. 해 뜨는 동쪽에는 유리광정토가
있고요, 탄생을 상징하고 약사여래가 관장하지요. 부처가 되기
전에 원력보살이었을 때 법장 비구가 마흔여덟 가지의 대원력을
세웠어요. 그 중에 죽음에 임해서라도 아미타부처님의 명호를
간절히 열 번만 부르는 중생이 있으면 이 정토에 태어나게 하리
라고 했지요.

F: 그건 "자등명自燈明 법등명法燈明 하라"는 부처님의 가르침과는
다르지 않나요?

K: 해탈에 이르는 한 방편으로 불보살님들의 가피력에 의지하는 타
력신앙이라고 할 수 있어요.

서방 극락정토는 어디에 있을까? 정淨을 형용사로 보면(pure land), 십
만억 국토를 지나 서방에 있다는 서(타)방정토설-타력신앙이 되고, 동
사로 보면(purify), 유마경의 '마음청정 국토청정'이 되어 유심정토설-자
력신앙이 된다. 일견 서로 대립적으로 보이는데, 자력으로 정토를 실
현할 수 없는 범부 중생을 위한 부처님의 자비교설이 아닌가!

5. Supreme Bliss Hall/ Infinite Life Hall/ Infinite Light Hall 2

극락전/무량수전/무량광전 2

F: How come you've stressed buddhism is the religion of practicing of self-power and individual responsibility?

K: Well, this could be explained in the Mahayana ideal. Mahayana emphasizes benefiting oneself and others. If sentient beings have firm faith in the vows of the Buddhas and Bodhisattvas and rely on their great power, they can be liberated and be reborn in the Pure Land of supreme Bliss. How could Buddhas and Bodhisattvas neglect those earnest prayers of beings?

F: Do you mean being reborn in the Pure Land is the same as being enlightened?

K: No. It is not the same. Even beings in the Pure Land, we call them gods or devas, when their virtuous merits are exhausted, they could be reborn into another of the 6 realms of the transmigratory.

F: Then, they too practice in paradise as we do here.

K: But since they are too happy enjoying their happiness and privilege, they never give mind to the suffering of others. We are frequently told by monks that this life is the best opportunity to escape from the cycle of birth and death,

when we take a human body. That's why monks always put
emphasis on 'practice and practice.'

F: 그럼 여태까지 불교는 자력적인 종교라고 강조한 얘기와는 어떻
게 되는 거죠?

K: 그건 대승불교의 이상으로 설명할 수 있지 않을까 싶어요. 대승
에서 강조하는 것이 자리이타自利利他거든요. 신심이 깊은 중생
이 불보살님께 의지하고 기도하면 불보살님들의 원력으로 해탈
하여 불국정토에 태어나는 거지요. 불보살님들이 어찌 중생들의
간절한 기도를 무시하겠어요.

F: 그럼 정토에 태어나는 것이 깨달음을 얻는 것과 같은가요?

K: 아니지요. 정토에 태어난 중생을 불교에서는 신(디바)이라 부르

Infinite Life Hall, 무량수전(부석사)

는데요, 그들도 복락이 다하면 다시 육도에 태어날 수 있어요.

F: 그럼 극락에서도 여기서 하듯 수행해야 되네요.

K: 그런데 그곳의 복락을 누리느라 다른 사람들의 고통에 관심을
안 갖는답니다. 그래서 스님들이 항상 말씀하시기를, 사람 몸 받
았을 때가 윤회에서 벗어날 수 있는 가장 좋은 기회라고 말씀하
시면서 수행할 것을 강조하는 것 같아요.

Amitabha's descent to welcome the dead,
아미타 내영도(혜담 스님 그림)

6. Triads: Matching Statues
삼존 형식: 불상 조성

With the rise of Mahayana, many different Bodhisattvas appeared on the scene; Avalokitesvara, Manjusuri, Ksitigarba, Maitreya, and so on. Various bodhisattvas statues were placed on the main altar with the Buddha. A sort of pattern – disposition and personalities chosen applies to place them.

The most common system is called triads. In general, Buddhist triads are composed of patterns such as Three Buddhas, one Buddha and two Bodhisattvas or one Buddha and two historical personages. The principally honored Buddha (주존불) varies with his accompanied images. When Virocana Buddha (법신, Dharmakaya) is in the center, Amitabha is to the left as Sambhogakaya (보신), and Sakyamuni is to the right as Nirmanakaya (화신). This is called the Buddhist Trinity or the threefold body of a Buddha (삼신불).

Often the Buddhas of the three time periods (삼세불), ie, past, present, and future, are placed; Sakyamuni is in the middle, between the Buddha of the Past (Dipamkara) and the Buddha of the Furure (Maitreya). Another triad shows that Sakyamuni Buddha is featured in the center with Amitabha in the Pure Land of Western Paradise (서방정토) and Medicine Buddha (Bhaisajyaguru) in the Pure Land of Lapis Lazuli Light (동방 유리

Sakyamuni is flanked by Ananda and Kasyapa,
아난다, 가섭존자 협시의 석가모니불(동국사)

광정토) on either side.

Each Buddha would be attended by their respective Bodhisattvas. Traditionally, Sakyamuni is accompanied by the Bodhisattvas Samantabadhara (보현보살, Universal Practice), and Manjusri (문수보살, Wisdom) or is flanked by his two disciples, Ananda and Kasyapa. This depiction is most commonly found in the Supportive Scroll Painting(탱화) behind the Buddaha image. Another combination is Amitabha Buddha attended by Avalokitesvara Bodhisattva (관세음보살, Compassion) and Mahastamprata Bodhisattva (대세지보살, Great Power). Medicine Buddaha's (약사여래) attendants are Sun and Moon Light Bodhisattvas (월광, 일광보살).

A Triad of Buddha allows us to pay respect to 3 different Buddhas in the same place without having to go to different halls.

대승불교가 발달하면서 관세음, 문수, 지장, 미륵 등의 여러 보살들이 출현하였다. 이에 보살들도 자연히 불단에 부처님과 함께 봉안 되었는데, 일종의 규칙성이 따랐다.

가장 보편적인 방식이 삼존 형식이다. 즉 삼불을 모시거나 한 부처님 양 옆에 두분의 보살이나 역사적 인물 두 분을 봉안하는 방식이다. 삼신불 봉안은 주존불로 비로자나불(법신)을 모시고 좌우에 아미타불(보신)과 석가모니불(화신)을 모시는 것이다. 시간적으로 과거(연등불), 현재(석가모니불), 미래(미륵불)의 삼세의 부처님을 봉안하면 삼세불 봉안이 된다. 공간적으로는 석가모니불 좌우에 서방정토 아미타불과 동방유리광정토 약사불을 모시기도 한다.

모든 부처님은 나름의 협시 보살(주불 좌우에 계신 보살)이 있는데 전통적으로는 석가모니불은 보현보살과 문수보살이, 또는 제자 중의 아난다와 가섭존자가 협시한다. 불상 뒤를 장엄하는 후불탱화에서는 대개 아난다와 가섭존자의 협시를 볼 수 있다. 관세음보살과 대세지보살은 아미타불의 협시보살이고 약사여래불의 협시보살은 월광과 일광보살이다.

삼존불께 참배하는 것은 한 공간에서 세 분의 부처님께 귀의/예배드리는 의미가 있다.

7. Judgment Hall with Ten Kings

명부전/지장전

K: No matter how small a temple is, there's almost always a Judgment Hall in addition to the Main Hall. Most funeral and memorial rituals are held at this hall. Many tourists are interested in this hall.

F: Why is that?

K: You'll see it. The Bodhisattva of Hell, Ksitigarbha, is enshrined with ten kings of Bardo here. You can recognize the Ksitigarbha Bodhisattva easily because of his green hair like a monk.

F: Those ten statues? There seems to be more than 10.

K: The Kings are sitting on the chairs. The pictures on the wall shows the hells that the kings govern. Other statues around the kings are attendants carrying brushes and papers on which the punishments or judgements are written.

F: What judgments?

K: The kings are judges who determine one's way after death according to one's actions in this life, reflected in the mirror. Ksitigarbha Bodhisattva stands next to the mirror and defends the dead. He made a great vow to put off his enlightenment until every being in hell is saved.

Ksitigarbha Bodhisattva in Judgment Hall, 지장보살

K: 작은 절이라고 할지라도 거의 대웅전 법당과 함께 있는 것이 명
   부전이죠. 장례식이나 천도재는 여기서 지내요. 외국인들이 여
   길 재미있어 해요.

F: 왜죠?

K: 지옥을 관장하는 지장보살과 시왕(十王)들이 여기 모셔져 있기
   때문일 거예요. 지장보살은 스님같아 보이는 파란 머리 때문에
   쉽게 알아볼 수 있어요.

F: 열 분의 상이요? 열 분보다 더 많은 것 같은데요.

K: 의자에 앉아 계시는 분들이 시왕이고요, 벽에 있는 그림은 그 시
   왕들이 다스리는 지옥 그림이에요. 옆에 있는 동자들은 판결문
   을 적을 붓과 종이를 들고 있어요.

F: 무슨 판결문이요?

K: 시왕들은 사람이 죽으면 이생에서의 업(행위)에 따라 다음 생을 결정하는 판관들이죠. 거울에 그 사람의 일생이 전부 비춰지거든요. 지장보살님은 거울 옆에 서서 죽은 사람을 변호하고 계시지요. 그분은 지옥 중생이 모두 구원될 때까지 성불을 미루겠다는 원을 세우셨지요.

Ten Kings in Judgment Hall, 명부전의 시왕(보광사)

8. Arhats' Hall
나한전/응진전

K: This is Disciples' Hall of Arhats. We call it the *nahan jeon* in Korean.

F: Who is arhat?

K: Arhat means 'worthy' and the Buddha was called arhat in the early Buddhist era and modern Theravadan tradition. These days the term is usually used to refer to personal disciples of Sakyamuni Buddha.

F: Then what is the difference between an arhat and a bodhisattva?

K: The ideal of arhat emphasizes personal attainment of enlightenment in Theravadan tradition. The bodhisattvas, on the other hand, dedicate themselves to benefitting others rather than their own enlightenment. Mahayana Buddhism places much less importance on the arhats than on the bodhisattvas. Therefore, in Korean temples, the arhats are usually enshrined in groups of 16, 18, 500 or 1250 rather than individually.

F: I think there must be some meaning with those figures.

K: 16 arhats were disciples of the Buddha who were ordered to disseminate Buddha's teaching after the Buddha's death. When two patrons were counted, it became 18.

500 refers arhats who attended the First Council which was called up for compiling of Sutra. The figure of 1250 refers congregated monks when the Buddha delivered the Diamond Sutra at the Anathapindika Park in Sravasti. Korean Buddhists like to pray in this hall because, I think, praying to those arhats who look familiar and friendly might help their wishes come true soon.

K: 여기는 나한전입니다.

F: 아라한(나한)은 누구를 말하나요?

K: 응공(공양을 받을 분)이라는 뜻이죠. 초기불교나 현대의 남방불교에서 아라한은 최고로 이상적인 깨달은 분, 즉 부처님을 그렇게 불렀어요. 오늘날에는 보통 석가모니 부처님의 제자들을 그렇게 지칭해요.

F: 그러면 보살과 나한은 어떻게 다르죠?

K: 남방(상좌부) 불교의 아라한은 개인의 성불을 강조하는 반면 대승불교의 보살은 이타에 중점을 두지요. 대승불교에서는 보살보다 나한을 별로 중요하게 생각하지 않았어요. 그래서 한국 절에서는 나한님들이 단독으로보다는 16나한, 500나한, 1250나한 등과 같이 집단으로 모셔지고 있어요.

F: 그렇다면 그 숫자에 의미가 있을 것 같은데요.

K: 16나한은 부처님 사후에 불법 전수를 부촉받은 제자 16분을 말하고, 거기에 두 분의 후원자를 포함한 숫자가 18이고요, 500은 제1차 결집에 모였던 나한님들이고요, 1250은 부처님이 사위성

Arhats' Hall, 나한전(보광사)

기수급고독원에서 『금강경』을 설하셨을 때 모인 회중을 말합니
다. 한국의 불자들은 나한전에서 기도드리는 것을 좋아해요. 나
한님들의 친근한 표정을 보면서 기도드리면 곧 기도가 이루어질
것 같은 생각이 들기 때문이 아닐까 생각해요.

9. Other Halls and Shrines

그밖의 전각들

Hall of Medicine Buddha: Bhaisajyaguru Hall (약사전)

The Mecicine Buddha is in the Eastern Paradise, the Pure Land of Lapis Lazuli Light (동방유리광정토). He has vowed to cure all diseases, to lengthen the lives of beings, and wipe out disasters. The Buddha holds a medicine bowl in his hand. Bhaisajyaguru is attended by two bodhisattvas of Sun and Moon (일광, 월광보살). When a family member gets sick, people go to the Medicine Buddha Hall and pray for a speedy recovery.

Medicine Buddha, 약함을 들고 있는 약사부처님

Daejeokgwangjeon Hall, 대적광전

Hall of Great Peace and Light (Hall of Great Illumination) (대적광전)

Virocana Buddha is enshrined as the central figure, sometimes flanked by Sakyamuni and Locana as Three Bodies of the

Buddha in this hall. Virocana is cosmic Buddha, the main figure in the Avatamsaka Sutra. This Buddha is identified by his knowledge fist mudra; enveloping the left thumb with the right hand.

Virocana Buddha, 비로자나불(봉암사)

Maitreya Hall (미륵전/용화전)

A hall dedicated to Maitreya Bodhisattva, guaranteed to be the next Buddha in this saha world after 567 billion years. He resides in Tusita Heaven awaiting the ending of his life as a Bodhisattva. Tusita Heaven is the fourth realm of Kamadhatu (world of desire 욕계). 'Maitreya' means benevolent or compassionate.

Patriarchs Shrine (조사당)

The shrine houses portraits of great patriarchs or the founder of the temple or its lineage. Memorial services for these renowned monks are performed here.

Patriarchs Hall, 조사전(화엄사)

Three Sages Shrine (삼성각)

The three sages are often placed together in one shrine, but sometimes separately. The Three Sages are Seven Star Dipper, Mountain Spirit, and Hermit-saint or Sravaka. Seven Star Dipper comes from Korean folklore, and Koreans consider it to be in charge of longevity of beings, especially the birth of babies and their healthy growth. Mountain Spirit is also indigenous, being worshiped as a protector of family and village from long before Buddhism reached Korea. He is depicted in a painting as an old man with a tiger or sitting on a tiger.

Hermit-saint was originally Indian arhats who attained arhatship alone, deep in mountains before the Buddha came to this world, being regarded as somewhat similar to the mountain god and expected to bring happiness to sentient beings.

Mountain Spirit with a tiger,
산신과 호랑이

10. Eight Scenes from the Buddha's Life
팔상도

These paintings are found in the Eight Paintings Hall (팔상전) or on the outside walls of the Main Hall. The paintings depict the eight most important events in the Buddha's life.

The scenes begin in the small kingdom ruled by King Suddhodana in the foothills of the Himalaya, Northern India, in the 6th century before Christ. Gautama was family name.

1/ Queen Maya had the auspicious dream of a white elephant and it seemed to enter her womb. Elephants are associated with rain or water in Indian mythology. (Descent from Tusita Heaven: 도솔래의상)

2/ The child was born at the Lumbini Garden on the way to the Queen's parents' home. The child was named Siddhartha, which means "one who has accomplished his aim." (Birth in the Lumbini Garden: 비람강생상)

3/ The prince went outside the palace and saw a sick man, an old man, a dead man and a mendicant. He was confronted with the reality of life and the suffering of mankind. (Four Encounters: 사문유관상)

4/ The prince left the palace and renounced worldly life to find the solution. (Renunciation: 유성출가상)

1   2   3

The Eight Great Events

5/ The Prince practiced austerities following famous religious teachers for 6 years. He became only skin and bones, and finally fainted. He recovered by an offering of milk porridge from Sujata. He made a vow to find the solution all by himself. (Ascetic Life: 설산수도상)

6/ After overcoming demons and temptations, at the age of 35, he attained full Enlightenment, looking at a rising star before dawn under the Bodhi tree, in Bodhgaya. (Resistance to the Mara: 수하항마상)

7/ He gave the First Dharma Discourse to 5 monks at the Deer Park at Sarnath. We call this first sermon 'Turning of the Wheel of the Dharma (전법륜)'; it contains essential teachings known as the Four Noble Truths (사성제). (Sermon in the Deer Park: 녹원전법상)

4   5   6

8/ The Buddha passed away at age of 80 between two sala trees at Kusinara. The buddha did not appoint a successor but advised his followers to strive on with diligence, relying on the self and Dharma. (Parinirvana: 쌍림열반상)

8상도는 팔상전이라는 독립 전각이나 대웅전 외벽에 그려지는데 부처님의 생애 중 가장 중요한 사건들을 묘사하고 있다. 북인도 히말라야 기슭의 작은 왕국에서 시작된다. 그때 왕은 슈도다나이고 씨족의 이름은 고타마이다. 기원 전 6세기 경이다.

1/ **도솔래의상**: 마야 왕비의 몸으로 흰 코끼리를 타고 이 세상에 오시다. 흰코끼리는 인도 설화에서 비, 물의 상서로움을 나타낸다.

2/ **비람강생상**: 룸비니 동산에서 태어나시다. '모든 것을 다 이루었

7   8

다'라는 뜻의 싯달타라고 이름을 짓다.

3/ **사문유관상**: 성문 밖에서 병들고, 늙고, 죽는 현실세계와 출가 수
행자의 평온을 목격하시다.

4/ **유성출가상**: 한 밤중에 성을 나와 출가를 하시다.

5/ **설산수도상**: 6년 동안 고행 수행을 치열하게 하시다가 결국 기절
하셨다. 수자타의 우유죽을 공양 받으시고 스스로 깨칠 것을 결
심하시다.

6/ **수하항마상**: 마왕의 항복을 받고 보리수 아래에서 새벽별을 보면
서 완전한 깨달음을 이루시다.

7/ **녹원전법상**: 녹야원에서 다섯 비구에게 사성제 설법으로 최초의
법륜을 굴리시다.

8/ **쌍림열반상**: 80세까지 길 위에서 전법하시다가 쿠시나가라 사라

쌍수 아래에서 열반에 드시다. 부처님은 후계자를 정하지 않았으며 다만 자신과 법(가르침)에 의지하여 정진할 것을 당부하셨다.

Four Noble Truths (4성제)

1) Suffering (Dukkha): Life is suffering. We have to endure not only physical but also mental suffering. : 고성제苦聖諦
2) The Causes of Suffering: Three poisons that are craving (attachment), anger (aversion) and ignorance (stupidity) are cause of suffering. : 집성제集聖諦
3) The Cessation of Suffering: can be attained by eliminating three poisons. : 멸성제滅聖諦
4) The Eightfold Path to the cessation of Suffering; the Eightfold Path: 도성제道聖諦

Eightfold Path (8정도)

Right understanding 正見/ Right thought 正思/ : *wisdom*
Right speech 正語/ Right action 正業/ Right livelihood 正命/ :
ethical conduct
Right Effort 正精進/ Right mindfulness 正念/ Right concentration
禪定/ : *concentration*

Last message entering into Parinirvana (자등명, 법등명)

Make yourself a light. Rely upon yourself: do not depend upon anyone else. Make my teachings your light. Rely upon them: do not depend upon any other teaching.

Part 5

Templestay Activities

1. What is Templestay Program?

템플스테이란?

When you are sick and tired of everyday routine in the midst of the hustle and bustle of city life, it is no wonder you desire to escape from it and have sometime to relax. Plus, if you could find the right place just by clicking on the internet, what a relief it would be. A Templestay Program at tranquil Korean Temples surrounded by nature in the deep mountains helps you refresh and reflect on life. Please come and join this program to be a friend with nature – with the sounds of water and wind.

Templestay Program started in the year of the 2002 Korea/ Japan World Cup, the first to be held in Asia, opening at only 33 temples to supplement accomodations and to introduce Korean traditional temple culture only for foreign visitors. Since then the government has aided renovattions to the accomodations, cooking and bathroom facilities of temples, it has settled successfully, and about 140 temples take part in welcoming domestic non-buddhists as well as foreign tourists today.

Usual programs are held through the weekend, beginning on Saturday afternoon and ending Sunday at noon. Basic programs include morning and evening chanting ceremonies (*yebul*), sitting meditation (*chamson*), talking with a venerable over tea (*dado*), making small lotus lanterns and a temple tour. However, programs vary depending on the tradition of the temple, and own distinctive programs are being developed, for instance, cooking temple food, natural dyeing, or paper crafts, etc,. Participants should keep in mind that attending the early morning and evening ceremony is required.

Some city temples in Seoul offer TempleLife Program for busy foreign tourists. It is a short version of the Templestay that lasts only 2 or 3 hours in the afternoon. This is available to the minimum of 5 persons by reservations in advance.

* the site of Templestay information is: support@templestay.com
  (Tel: 82-2-2031-2000)

소란스러운 도시 생활의 반복되는 일상에 지쳐갈 때 단 하루라도 일상에서 벗어나 편히 쉴 수 있는 곳이 어디 없을까 고민하면서, 인터넷에 들어가서 클릭 몇 번으로 딱 맞춤의 장소를 찾을 수 있다면 얼마나 좋을까? 고요한 산사에서 자연을 벗 삼아 물소리 바람소리 들으며 일상을 되돌아보고 재충전을 할 수 있는 기회가 바로 템플스테이 프로그램이다.

템플스테이는 2002년 한국과 일본이 공동 주최국으로 월드컵 경기가 열리면서 시작되었다. 당시에는 외국인 방문객의 부족한 숙박시설을 보충하기 위해 우선 33곳의 사찰이 지정되었다. 그 후 정부의 지원으로 숙박시설은 물론 화장실과 조리실 등이 개선되고 정착되면서 현재는 140여 개 사찰에서 진행하고 있다. 불자, 비불자를 가리지 않고 내국인 누구에게나 개방되어 있으며, 외국인을 위한 사찰 또한 따로 지정되어 있다.

주로 주말 오후에 시작하여 일요일 점심 공양 후에 해산한다. 아침, 저녁 예불 참석, 참선, 스님과의 다담, 작은 연등이나 염주 만들기, 사찰 경내 소개 등이 기본 프로그램이며, 사찰의 특성에 따라 다양한 프로그램들을 개발하여 진행하고 있다. 예를 들면 사찰음식 만들기, 자연염색 하기, 한지 공예 등을 포함하고 있다. 반드시 유념할 점은 아침, 저녁 예불은 권장사항이 아니라 필수라는 점이다.

서울에 있는 몇몇 절에서는 바쁜 외국인 관광객을 위해서 주로 오후에 두 시간 내지 세 시간짜리 짧은 템플스테이 프로그램을 운영하기도 한다. 이는 동참자가 다섯 사람 이상이어야 하고, 사전예약을 해야 한다.

2. Templestay Schedule
템플스테이 일정

[2 days / 1 night program]

<first day>

14:00   Arrival and Registration 도착과 등록
        (handing out uniforms and assigning rooms)
        수련복 지급과 방 배정

15:00   Opening Ceremony 개회식

16:00   Temple Tour 사찰 안내

18:00   Dinner (Baru Offering) 저녁 공양(바루공양)

19:00   Evening Yebul 저녁예불

19:30   Tea Ceremony-talking with Sunim over tea 다도:
        스님과 대화

20:30   Making a bed 취침준비

21:00   Sleep – light out 취침 – 소등

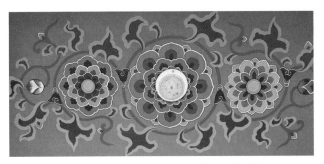

lotus pattern at cosmic design, 연꽃 문양 단청

\<second day\>

03:30   Morning Yebul 아침예불

04:00   Meditation 참선

06:00   Breakfast 아침공양

07:00   Group Work 울력

08:00   Special program depending on temples
         절에 따른 프로진행

11:00   Closing Ceremony 폐회식

12:00   Lunch 점심공양

13:00   Departure 출발

(This is a general schedule for an overnight program. Details and activities vary according to each temple's situation.)

3. Yebul: Pay Homage to the Buddha
예불

F: I'm afraid I won't be able to get up so early tomorrow morning.

K: No worries. You may have no choice but to wake up.

A monk walks around to every corner of the temple compound, hitting a *moktak* and chanting to wake up all beings. We call it *Doryangsuk,* waking up chant. Then, the sounds of four instruments; first, Dharma drum, then wooden fish, cloud gong, and Dharma bell follows in order.

F: Then I'm relieved.

K: All the Templestay participants along with temple residents should gather in the Main Buddha Hall before the sound of Dharma bell ends. In any Korean temples, daily routine begins with this morning Yebul, the first communal chant, which pays homage to the Sakyamuni Buddha, Bodhisattvas, Disciples and Patriarchs, and to pray that all sentient beings in the universe be well and happy.

F: Does it take long?

K: No, it usually lasts less than 20 minutes.

Even though you do not understand the whole meaning of the Yebul sentences, you'll feel solace and solemn just hearing the intoning voices in unison. Actually I like this morning chant the most among three times chants in a day. I feel really happy that I'm here in a temple at this time, walking under the starry sky and paying homage to the Buddha. I'd like to make sure you know that it is mandatory to attend morning and evening Yebul.

F: 내일 아침 일찍 일어날 수 있을지 걱정이 돼요.

K: 걱정 말아요. 일어날 수밖에 없어요. 스님이 목탁 치며 염불하면서 경내 구석구석을 다니는 도량석을 도니까요. 그러고 나면 사물 소리가 법고, 목어, 운판, 범종의 순서로 울려 퍼져요.

F: 그렇다면 안심이에요.

K: 절 식구들이나 템플스테이 참석자들 모두는 범종소리가 끝나기 전에 법당에 모여야 돼요. 한국의 모든 절의 하루는 예불로 시작되지요. 부처님, 보살님들, 제자들과 조사스님들께 예경드리며

Yebul, 예불

모든 중생의 행복을 기원하면서 하루를 시작하는 것입니다.

F: 예불이 오래 걸리나요?

K: 아니요, 보통 20분 이내에 끝나요. 예불문의 의미를 전부 몰라도 장엄한 예불소리에 위안과 엄숙함을 느낄 수 있을 거예요. 사실 난 아침예불을 제일 좋아해요. 아직 별이 총총한 하늘을 바라보며 이 시각에 절에서 예불드릴 수 있는 것이 정말 행복하다고 느껴지거든요. 템플스테이 참가자들에게는 아침저녁 예불 참석이 필수 사항임을 잊지 말아요.

4. Sitting Meditation: Posture and Breathing
좌선: 기본 자세와 호흡

Hwadu meditation, called *ganhwaseon* in Korean is the representative practice in Korean Buddhism. Hwadu is a key subject that keeps generating great doubt about the nature of existence and true self that cannot be solved by intellect, and it is given by a great monk (큰스님). In my experience it is for spiritually high-capacity beings, not ordinary beings like me.

So today, I recommend a meditation focusing on your breath: counting your breaths to focus your mind. This practice could be a basis of *hwadu* meditation later. An inhale and an exhale is counted as one breath. The breathing should be 'a deep-long, yet thin and even through nose.' When you breath in, your belly rises, when you breath out, your belly falls. As a beginner, to collect your mind, you should focus on this motion of the falling and rising abdomen. Try to make your inhale short and exhale long. Count your breaths up to 10 and repeat it.

Let go of thoughts and emotions, whatever arise, and bring your attention back to your breath, not clinging to nor following your thoughts. Actually hundreds of thousands of thoughts come up, possibly disturbing your attention. It is no wonder because this is your first chance to focus on something solely. This experience in comings and goings of deluded thoughts is all the same as you do other practice like bowing, chanting, or dharani recitation at first. It will take some time to experience some peace and stillness. So do not give up, just keep up with it. This means you should pay attention to what you are doing 'here and now', and this could lead you to focus and control your mind in daily life in the end.

There are two lotus postures: the full and the half lotus posture. The full lotus posture is to make your two legs cross each other by putting your right foot on your left thigh and the left foot on the right thigh. The half lotus posture is easier than the full lotus posture, raising only one foot onto the other thigh. This posture makes your back straight. This is the most essential point of posture. Make your cushion a bit higher

Sitting Meditation, 좌선

under your buttocks; this helps you more easily keep your back erect. Eyes half open to prevent drowsiness, look one meter ahead of you. When you fall drowsy or break posture, the *sunim* will pat your shoulder with a *jukbi* to let you know that *sunim* is going to admonish you. Then you show *hapjang*, and turn your head toward the opposite shoulder. After the *sunim* taps your shoulder with the stick, do *hapjang* to show gratitude. Then go back to meditation.

Generally, meditation begins with 3 claps of the *jukbi* and lasts 40 or 50 minutes. When the *jukbi* claps 2 times, one period ends and a 10-minutes walking meditation follows to relax and stimulate the blood circulation.

우리말로 간화선이라고 하는 화두참선은 한국불교 조계종의 대표적인 수행법이다. 화두란 지적으로는 해결할 수 없는 존재의 본질을 참구할 때 계속 의정을 일으키게 하는 주제로, 큰스님한테서 (화두를) 받는다. 그런데 내 경험으로는 화두참선은 나같은 평범한 사람보다는 근기가 수승한 사람을 위한 것이란 생각이다.

그래서 오늘은 호흡에 집중하는 명상을 소개하려고 한다. 나중에 화두참선을 할 수 있는 기초가 될 수 있다. 들이쉬는 호흡(입식)과 내쉬는 호흡(출식)이 한 호흡이다. '코로 호흡하되, 길고 깊게, 고르게 숨쉬기'가 기본이다. 들이쉴 때 아랫배가 올라오고, 내쉴 때 꺼진다. 초심자는 복부의 오르고 내림에 마음을 모으는 것이 도움이 된다. 조금 익숙해지면 '들이쉬기는 짧게, 내쉬기를 길게(입식 단, 출

식 장)' 하도록 노력하면서 호흡을 하나에서 열까지 헤아리고 다시
반복한다.

호흡이 제법 고르게 된다 싶으면, 이 생각 저 생각이 떠올라 머
리를 어지럽힌다. 소위 망상이다. 이때 망상들에 계속 끄달려 이리
저리 생각을 굴리지 말고, 알아차리고 곧 호흡으로 돌아와 하나, 둘
세면서 호흡에 집중한다. 살아오면서 오직 한 가지에 집중해 본 적
이 별로 없었는데 처음으로 가만히 앉아 해보고 있으니 이런 현상
이 일어나는 것이 당연하다. 이런 현상은 절, 염불, 주력 등 다른 수
행을 할 때도 마찬가지이다. 고요한 마음 상태로 되기까지는 시간
이 걸린다. 그러니 망상 때문에 못하겠다고 포기하지 말아야 한다.
이는 '지금, 여기'에 집중하는 훈련이 되어 일상에서 산란한 마음을
집중하고 조절하는 데 도움이 될 수 있다.

참선 자세는 결가부좌와 반가부좌가 있다. 결가부좌는 오른쪽 다
리를 왼쪽 허벅지 위에 올려놓아 서로 교차하게 한다. 반가부좌는
결과부좌보다 쉬운데, 한쪽 다리만 다른 쪽 허벅지 위에 올려놓는
다. 이러한 자세들은 허리를 곧추 세우도록 하기 위함인데, 바로 참
선 자세에서 가장 강조되는 지점이다. 이를 위해 엉덩이 밑에 방석
을 높게 받쳐주면 도움이 된다. 졸면 안 되니까 눈은 감는 것보다
반쯤 뜨고 1미터쯤 떨어진 곳에 눈길을 둔다. 졸거나 자세가 흩어
지면 스님이 죽비로 어깨를 가볍게 쳐서 경책을 준다. 이때는 합장
을 하고 반대쪽으로 머리를 돌려 경책을 받는다. 받은 후에는 감사
의 표시로 합장을 하고 참선을 계속한다.

참선은 한 번 기간에 40분이나 50분 계속하고, 두 번 죽비 치는

소리가 들리면 일어나서 10분간 행선(포행: 걸으면서 하는 참선)을 하면서 다리를 풀어준다. 죽비 치는 소리가 세 번 들리면 자기 자리에 돌아가 참선을 계속한다.

5. What is Baru Offering (Communal Meal)?

바루(발우)공양이란?

Have you ever experienced Baru Offering which is mostly included in Templestay Program nowadays? Many may remember it as a very strict and stressful way of eating. However in buddhist culture, eating is not just nourishing this body but a way of practicing to reach the goal of enlightenment.

Baru is four wooden bowls used for monastic meals, especially at communal meals, which are mostly held in meditation halls. The four bowls can be stacked into one, and every monk has his own baru and takes it any temple he goes, in his knapsack.

Seon(Zen) monks who dedicate most of their time to meditation do not waste their time going to the dining room and coming back again to the meditation hall; food comes to them instead. Each monk sits with his baru in front of him on the floor, into which goes rice, soup, kimchi or vegetables and water. Everyone eats at the same time in total silence following the claps of bamboo stick (jukbi). Once the meal is finished, the monks wash their bowls with the water in their water baru and neatly re-pack the baru. No food is allowed to remain and no dishes remain to be washed. How nice and eco-friendly it is!

In Seon tradition, there's a saying that "Tea and Seon are the same taste. They are not different." Drinking tea is treated as Seon. How much more it can be with eating! So it could be said "eating and Seon are not different." This sort of idea can be read in the 'Gatha of Ohkwan' (five contemplations); the verse should be chanted just before eating, after foods has been distributed:

Where has this food come from?
Am I worthy of receiving this food?
Detaching all my desires
As a medicine to sustain my body
I will take it as an offering to attain enlightenment.

Just as all blessings of the universe caress each drop of water
The human effort in even a single grain is boundless.
I humbly take this food in gratitude
And as nourishment to serve all beings.

We live with excessively abundant food and materials these days, forgetting poor and hard times not long ago. How about chanting and keeping in mind these 'Five Contemplations' at every meal time at home and school? It will help us be rather modest in front of food and give thank for it.

(This was released in the English Buddhist magazine "Buddha Link" in 2006.)

Baru, 바루(펴기 전과 후)

바루(발우)공양을 해본 적이 있습니까? 요즈음 템플스테이 프로그램에 대부분 포함되어 있습니다. 아마도 해 본 사람들은 아주 어렵고 스트레스 받으며 밥을 먹었다고 기억할 수도 있습니다. 그러나이 공양법은 단지 우리 몸에 영양을 공급하는 것이 목적이 아니고 깨달음에 이르는 수행의 한 가지입니다.

발우는 네 개로 포개진 밥그릇을 말하는데, 주로 스님들이 선방에서 다함께 식사(공양)할 때 쓰는 도구를 말합니다. 선방스님들은 각자 자기 발우를 갖고 어느 절에 가든 가지고 다닙니다.

 결제 중의 선방스님들은 모든 시간을 참선에 전념해야 하는데, 밥 먹으러 식당으로 왔다 갔다 하면서 시간을 허비할 수 없으니까 그 대신에 밥이 스님들께 오는 것입니다. 어시(밥), 국, 반찬, 청수 발우를 각자의 발단 위에 펼쳐놓고 각자 먹을 수 있는 만큼의 밥과 음식을 덜어서 죽비 소리에 맞춰 정적 속에서 진행합니다. 식사가 끝나면 청수발우에 받아 두었던 물로 깨끗이 발우를 닦아서 다시 단정하게 싸야 합니다. 음식은 절대 남기면 안 되고 설거지 그릇이 남을 일도 없습니다. 그러니 얼마나 친환경적인 식사법인가요!

선방에서 스님들이 흔히 하는 말에 '다선일미茶禪一味'라는 말이 있습니다. 차 마시는 일이 선(수행)과 다르지 않다라는 뜻인데, 그러니 밥 먹는 일이야 더 말할 나위가 있을까요! 이런 사상은 오관게 게송에 잘 나타나 있습니다. 이 게송은 스님들이 음식을 전부 받고 먹기 시작 전에 다 같이 암송합니다.

"이 음식이 어디서 왔는가?
내 덕행으로는 받기가 부끄럽네.
마음의 온갖 욕심 버리고
육신을 지탱하는 약으로 알아
깨달음을 이루고자 이 공양을 받습니다."

"한 방울의 물에도 천지의 은혜가 스며 있고
한 알의 곡식에도 만인의 노고가 담겨 있습니다.
이 음식으로 배고픔을 달래고 몸과 마음을 바르게 하여
이웃과 세상에 보탬이 되겠습니다."

요즈음 우리는 음식이든 무엇이든 차고 넘치는 세상을 살고 있습니다. 배고프고 굶주리던 시절이 엊그제인데도 말입니다. 이제 가정에서, 학교에서 이 게송을 합송하고 나서 밥을 먹으면 음식에 좀 더 감사하고 겸손해지지 않을까요?

6. Baru Gongyang Practical Points
바루(발우)공양 실참

(Overview)

Baru gongyang is a monastic way of eating. When you say 'Gongyang' in a Korean temple, it has two meanings. One is offering things to the Buddha to show respect and gratitudes, and the other is eating a meal. Baru Gongyang is not just eating but practicing. Basic posture is the same as when you meditate, sitting in lotus or half lotus posture with your spine straight and palms together.

(개요)

바루공양은 절집에서 스님들이 식사하는 방법을 말한다. 공양이란 말은 절에서 부처님 전에 올리는 공물을 말하기도 하고, 단순히 밥 먹는 것을 뜻하기도 한다. 그러나 단순히 먹는 행위를 말하기보다 수행의 하나로 본다. 바루공양의 기본자세는 참선 자세와 같이 합장과 등을 곧추 세운 결가부좌 혹은 반가부좌이다.

(Three Rules)

At the time of Buddha, the Buddha himself entered the city to beg food holding one bowl, and he made 3 rules for mendicants.

1. The monks should have their food by begging. Why begging? Begging is the best way to get rid of their arrogant and self-centered mind.

2. When they beg, visit fewer than 7 houses and do not distinguish the poor or the rich, and get whatever food given. This is to give equal chances to make merits.

3. Take one meal in a day before noon. Do not eat in the afternoon.

(세 가지의 규정)

부처님께서도 당시에 손수 바루를 들고 마을로 가서서 공양을 받았다. 이때 규칙 세 가지를 정하셨다.

1. 스님들의 식사는 걸식으로 해결한다. 왜 하필 걸식일까? 걸식이 마음의 오만과 자기중심적인 사고에서 벗어날 수 있는 최선이라고 생각했기 때문이다.

2. 걸식 시에는 부잣집이나 가난한 집을 가리지 말고 가되 주는 대로 받아야 하고 일곱 집을 넘지 말아야 한다. 이는 적선의 기회를 고루 주기 위한 배려이다.

3. 오전 중의 한 끼 식사만 허용한다.

   오후에는 불식을 원칙으로 한다.

Theravadan countries have kept these rules so far. But these rules has changed a bit while Buddhism came to Korea through China. India is so hot that they can practice with one meal in a day. But in China and Korea, we have very bitterly cold winter. The monks can not keep enough energy with one meal. So we take three meals only with vegetarian diets and no spicy seasoning. Due to the characteristics of Korean food one bowl became four bowls.

남방불교권에서는 아직도 이 규칙을 지키고 있다. 그러나 중국을 거쳐 불교가 이 땅에 들어오면서 변화가 있었다. 기후가 더운 인도에서는 한 끼 식사로 건강을 유지하며 수행이 가능하지만 혹한의 겨울이 있는 한국에서는 어려운 일이었기 때문에 강한 양념을 쓰지 않은 담백한 채식 위주의 식단으로 바뀌었고, 국물이 있는 한국음식의 특성상 한 개의 바루가 네 개로 바뀌었다.

(Table manners)

1. Please keep in mind that you are not allowed to leave any food. Take the amount of food that you can eat up.
2. Acting together is important. Try to keep pace with others. The whole procedure of eating is regulated by a head monk with a bamboo stick without saying a single word except for some recitation.
3. Do not eat like you are sitting at a dining table. It means everytime you eat, you lift the bowl up to your mouth and then put it down.
4. Do not mix anything in the rice bowl. In the rice bowl, there should be rice and a piece of kimchi or radish to clean all bowls at the end of meal. But you can mix everything in the soup bowl.
5. After you use chopsticks, you rest them on the water bowl,

not put them in the water. This is to keep the water clean. After using your spoon, you put it in the soup bowl.

6. Save one piece of Kimchi or radish in the side of rice bowl. This is going to be used for cleaning the bowls at the end of meal.

7. Try to keep the water clean; The water you receive at the beginning should be kept clean until the end of the meal. Water in the end should be almost as clean as the water at the beginning.

(바루공양 예절)

1. 음식은 조금도 남기면 안 되므로 다 먹을 수 있는 양만큼만 덜어 먹는다.

2. 단체 행동이 중요하기 때문에 다른 사람들과 보조를 맞춰야 한다. 게송을 할 때 외에는 말하지 않는다. 모든 절차는 죽비소리로

Baru Gongyang, 바루공양

진행한다.

3. 식탁에 앉아 식사하듯이 하면 안 된다. 이는 먹을 때마다 바루를 입으로 가져가서 먹고 내려놓기를 반복한다.

4. 밥바루(어시바루)에는 밥과 김치나 무 한 조각 외에는 어떤 것도 섞으면 안 된다. 김치나 무 한 조각은 나중에 바루를 씻을 때 쓰기 위한 것이다. 그러나 국바루에는 반찬을 섞어도 된다.

5. 젓가락은 사용한 후 청수바루(속에 넣지 말고)에 걸쳐 놓는다. 숟가락은 국바루에 넣어도 된다. 이는 물을 끝까지 깨끗하게 하기 위함이다.

6. 김치나 무 한 조각은 어시바루 안쪽에 남겨두어서 설거지를 할 때 쓴다.

7. 공양 처음 시작할 때 청수바루에 받은 물이 공양 끝난 후에도 깨끗해야 한다.

7. Tea Ceremony
다도

(overview)

You may wonder if having a cup of tea is really a Tea Ceremony or Tea Way. "All roads lead to Rome." is a famous saying. We can apply this in Buddhism like "all actions lead to practice." While you are brewing tea, if you do not pay attention to every procedure, you cannot produce and maintain balanced flavor, color and aroma of tea. Therefore there is a saying that 'Tea and Seon meditation have the same taste (다선일미).' It means making tea is another mindfulness practice.

차 한 잔 마시는 것이 무슨 다도라고까지 말하나 라는 생각을 할 수도 있다. 그러나 모든 길은 로마로 통한다는 말이 있듯이 절집에서는 모든 행위는 수행으로 통한다라고 말할 수 있다. 차를 우릴 때 그 과정마다 집중하지 않으면 향기와 색이나 맛을 제대로 낼 수가 없기 때문이다. 그래서 다선일미 "차와 선은 같은 맛이다"라는 말이 있다. 즉 차를 만드는 일 또한 정념 (마음 집중) 수행인 것이다.

(Tea and Buddhism)

Tea seems to have been introduced in the sixth or seventh centuries, along with the dissemination of Buddhism from

China to Korea.

In Buddhism, offering tea is one of six offerings to the Buddha, they are tea, incense, lantern, flower, fruit, and rice. After the Buddha entered into Parinirvana tea was offered on the alter in front of a stupa which contained relics of the Buddha. However, we have a tradition of offering clean well-water on an altar for Dangun, who was the founder of Korea. This tradition mixed with the tea offering to the Buddha and formed a refined, unique tea tradition in Korea. The tea ceremony developed through the Silla and Koryo Dynasties when Buddhism flourished as a nation-protecting religion. Since the Joseon Dynasty adopted Confucianism as an idea of establishment, oppressing Buddhism, the tea tradition almost disappeared. Fortunately it survived only by a great scholar, Chong Yak-yong, and Buddhist monk Cho-ui until early in the 19th century.

차는 6,7세기경에 불교와 함께 우리나라에 들어 온 것으로 알려져 있다. 차는 6법 공양물 중 하나이다. 부처님께서 열반에 드신 후에 는 사리탑 앞 제단에 차 공양을 올렸다. 우리민족에게도 단군 조상 님께 정화수를 올리는 오랜 전통이 있기에 쉽게 받아들여졌고 우 리만의 차 전통이 만들어졌다. 불교가 호국 불교 역할을 했던 신라, 고려조에서는 차 문화가 발달 했지만 억불 숭유의 조선조를 거치면 서 차문화는 거의 사라졌다. 다행하게도 정약용 선생과 초의 선사 에 의해 되살아났다.

Since the 1970s there has been a growing concern on our own tradition, many people have become interested in tea ceremony and developing our own style and trying to apply it to daily life. Koreans regard drinking and enjoying tea in a free and relaxed way whereas Japanese do it in a very rigid and complicated way.

1970년대를 지나면서 우리문화에 대한 관심이 높아지면서 우리 방식대로 차를 발전시키고 일상생활에 활용하기 시작했다. 일본에서의 차 생활은 매우 엄격하고 형식이 까다로운 반면에 우리는 편안하게 차를 즐긴다.

(Traditional tea set)
tea kettle: kettle for boiling water / 수주
tea brewing pot: hold water to brew tea / 다관
cooling bowl: to let water cool to 70-80 degrees / 숙우
tea cup / tea cloth / tea jar / tea scoop / 찻잔 / 다건 / 차호 / 차수저
waste water bowl: to hold water used in the tea pot and tea cup / 퇴수기
wooden saucer: a wooden saucer is preferable over ceramics as it does not make noise. / 목기 찻잔받침: 도기 받침보다 소리가 나지 않으므로 목기 받침을 권한다
tea covering cloth / 다건

(How to brew tea)
1. Natural mineral water is recommended for good tea; if tap

water, leave it out overnight. You can use the same tea leaves up to three times.

2. Boil mineral water in the kettle and pour some into the tea cups to warm them in advance.

3. Put tea leaves into the tea brewing pot. The proper quantity of tea leaves is 2 grams for each person.

4. Pour boiling water from the kettle into the cooling water bowl to cool down to 70-80C, then pour it into the tea brewing pot; water that is too hot or brewing for too long makes a bitter taste.

5. While the tea is brewing for 2 or 3 minutes, empty the water warming up the cups into the waste bowl.

6. To balance the color and taste of tea, fill each cup in three sequences; fill each cup one third full in descending order,

Tea Ceremony, 다도

one third full in ascending order and one third full in descending order.

7. Put each tea cup, one by one, on a saucer and serve it to the guest. Only one person moving at a time is the rule when it is served.

좋은 찻물은 광천수가 좋지만 수돗물인 경우는 하루쯤 지난 물이 좋다 물을 끓여 70도나 80도 정도로 식으면 찻잎을 넣는데 이는 물이 너무 뜨거우면 떫은맛이나 쓴맛이 나기 쉽기 때문이다. 한 사람당 약 2그램의 차가 적당하다. 찻잎은 두 번이나 세 번까지 우려 쓸수 있다. 차향과 맛과 색 또한 온도가 일정해야 하므로 차를 따를 때는 한 번에 잔을 채우지 않고 한 번에 삼분의 일씩 따라서 세 번에 나누어 잔을 채우도록 하여 차받침에 올려 대접한다.

(How to drink tea)
1. Hold the cup with your right hand with left hand supporting the bottom of the cup.
2. Give thanks to the host who serves the tea.
3. Drink the tea with three sips enjoying three things; the color with your eyes, the scent with your nose and flavor with your tongue.

차는 왼손으로 찻잔을 받치고 오른손으로 잔을 들고 마시되 세 번에 나누어 마시는데 첫째 모금은 입안을 적시는 정도로 마시면서 향기를 맡는다. 둘째 모금을 마시고 가슴까지 내려오는 맛을 음미하고 시선은 차의 색을 즐긴다.

(Cleaning tea set)

1. Collect the tea cups and place them on the table.

2. Take the tea leaves out of the pot.

   Pour hot water into the cooling bowl to clean cups.

3. Soak the rim of each cup in the water in the cooling bowl.

4. Clean the rims of the tea cups with the tea cloth.

5. Put the tea cups upside down to dry.

6. Empty the cooling bowl into waste bowl and replace it.

7. Cover the tea table with the table cloth.

찻잔을 거두어 찻상에 놓고 다관의 찻잎은 꺼내 모두 쏟는다.

숙우에 거둔 컵들을 넣고 뜨거운 물을 부어서 찻잔 가장자리를 주의해서 씻은 후 다건으로 물기를 닦고 엎어 놓는다. 숙우의 물도 퇴수기에 쏟아버리고 제자리에 놓는다. 찻상을 다건으로 씌워놓는다.

8. To be a Nun (Monk) in the Jogye Order
조계종 스님 되기

F: Those grey-robed ladies in the temple yard are nuns?

K: No. they are lay buddhists. You should notice the hair. Nuns shave off their hair.

F: Their gray robes mislead me. I heard Korea has kept a bhiksuni tradition alive.

K: Exactly. I knew some foreign bhiksunis who studied in Theravada Buddhist countries, then came to Korea to be ordained as a certified Bhiksuni.

F: As a woman, I am very curious about the course of being a nun. How long does it take to be a nun? Could you kindly share with me the educational process?

K: I only know the procedure involved in the Jogye Order. A candidate goes through 3 stages. The first stage is a kind of trial basis living in an actual temple for at least 5 months. During this period the aspirant, we call her *hangja* in Korean, does all the chores of the temple to adjust herself to the hard communal life physically first. She learns temple regulations and chanting as well. As this period is over, she is sent to a basic trainee's course for 3 or 5 weeks at a school. Upon its completion, the aspirant (*hangja*) takes postulant (*sramanera*) ordination (*samigye*), and becomes a preparatory Sunim (*samini*).

F: When does she shave her head? Soon after she enters the temple?

K: At that time is the male's case, but a female does it after finishing 5-months of living at the temple. As a novice, she has two chances. She can go to a monastic seminary, *kangwon* in Korean or *Sangha* college for 4 years for textual studying. If she is interested in meditation, she joins the Meditation Hall, *Seonwon* in Korean, mostly practicing *hwadu* meditation for 4 years. After at least 4 years living as a samini, the novice takes full ordination (*kujokgye: 250 precepts for monks and 348 precepts for nun*) to be an fully ordained bhiksuni/nun (*sunim*). Passing an examination is a requirement at every stage.

F: 저기 마당에 회색 옷 입은 여인들이 비구니 스님인가요?

K: 아니요 신도들입니다. 머리를 보면 알아요.

　　스님들은 머리를 깎지요.

F: 그렇군요. 회색 옷 때문에 그렇게 생각했어요.

　　그리고 한국에 비구니 승단이 있다고 들었거든요.

K: 맞아요. 남방불교에서 공부한 외국 여자 스님이 정식으로 계 받
　　으려고 한국에 오신 경우를 알고 있어요.

F: 스님에 관심이 많아요. 스님이 되려면 어떻게 해야 되지요?
　　얼마나 걸려요?

K: 조계종단의 과정만 얘기할게요. 3단계를 거치죠. 처음에 행자기

간은 적어도 5개월 이상을 절에서 생활하면서 절에서 온갖 궂은 일을 하면서 절 생활을 몸으로 익혀야 해요. 물론 절에서의 규범과 염불 등도 익히지요. 이 기간이 끝나면 3-5주간의 기본교육 과정의 공동 교육을 (학교에서) 이수하고 사미계를 받습니다. 사미나 사미니의 예비스님이 된 거지요.

F: 머리는 언제 깎나요? 절에 들어가자마자 깎나요?

K: 남자의 경우는 그때 깎지만 여자들은 5개월 지난 후에 깎아요. 사미계를 받으면 두 가지 길이 있어요. 강원에 가서 4년 동안 교학공부를 하든가, 참선에 관심 있으면 선원에 가서 4년간 화두 참선을 합니다. 어디서든 4년 과정을 마쳐야 구족계를 받고 정식 스님이 됩니다. 각 과정마다 시험을 치르고요.

회색 옷차림의 재가자들을 보고 스님으로 착각하는 외국인이 더러 있다. 재가자들이 입는 회색의 승복 비슷한 법복 차림에 평소 별 생각이 없었는데, 외국인들이 왜 재가자들이 스님 같은 옷을 입느냐고 의아해 하는 걸 보고 재고할 필요가 있다는 생각이다. 구족계를 받을 때 비구는 250계이고 비구니는 348계를 받는 것을 두고 불평등을 애기하는 사람이 있지만, 이는 부처님 당시 여성 수행자를 보호하기 위한 배려 차원에서 유래한 것이라고 한다.

The Five Precepts (오계)

I take the training rule of refraining from killing any living thing and I practice loving-kindness.

I take the training rule of refraining from taking anything that is not given and I practice generosity.

I take the training rule of refraining from sensual and sexual misconduct and I practice awareness.

I take the training rule of refraining from lying and bad speech and I practice wholesome speech.

I take the training rule of refraining from all intoxicants and I practice clear mindedness.

Ten Precepts (십계)

1) not to kill anything
2) not to take anything that is not given
3) to be celibate
4) not to lie
5) not to take intoxicants
6) not to eat outside of mealtimes
7) not to adorn himself
8) not to delight in singing, dancing or shows
9) not to seek comfort
10) not to amass wealth

5계는 재가자들이 보살계(bodhisattva precepts)를 받을 때 수지한다. 보살계는 스님들이나 재가자들이 많이 받을수록 좋다고 해서 자주 받기도 한다. 10계는 행자가 사미계 받을 때 수지하고 서약한다.

9. Jogye Order

조계종

F: You said you're a lay buddhist who belongs to the Jogye Order. What is the Jogye Order?

K: The Jogye Order is the largest, influential, and leading Order in Korea. More than 90 percent of lay buddhists belong to this Order. The Jogye Order supports Seon (Zen) meditation, as we have kept the tradition of the lineage of the sixth patriarch of Seon, Huineung, in China. However, chanting, dharani recitation, reading Sutras, and bowing are recommended to the laity as main disciplines along with meditation in most temples. The main text is the Diamond Sutra, but other sutras like Avatamsaka, Lotus, and Pure Land sutras are acknowledged and encouraged.

F: Then how many orders do you have?

K: Officially there are more than 30 Orders, but 5 are somewhat large orders, including the Jogye Order.

F: Then, how many buddhists are there in your population?

K: Let's say this. Half of the population is religious, and half of those religious people are buddhists.

F: What could you point out as the traits of the Jogye Order?

K: Well, I cannot but say roughly several traits. They are; monks keep celibacy, and vegetarian meals and they follow the tradition of three months of retreats in summer and winter. Above all, harmonization of doctrinal understanding and Seon meditation is the strong point of Korean Buddhism, including the Jogye Order.

F: How about churches in Korea? Churches in Western countries are declining these days.

K: It is not the same case in Korea. As you know, after the Korean War, we were divided into North and South. Under this insecure circumstances, the savior of the Almighty God worked well for the poor and hurt nation. With economic growth, those who studied overseas, mainly in America came back home and became government officials or politicians, and their policies favored Christianity. I think this is one of the reasons why Christianity, especially the Protestant church, is so prosperous in Korea.

F: 조계종단에 속한 불자라고 말했죠? 조계종은 뭔가요?

K: 한국불교에서 가장 크고 영향력 있는 종단이지요. 한국 불자의 90% 이상이 여기 소속입니다. 중국 선종의 6대 조사인 혜능 선사의 법맥을 계승하고 있기 때문에 수행법은 주로 참선을 강조하고 있지만 염불, 다라니, 간경, 절수행 등도 불자들한테 권장하고 있습니다.

F: 그럼 한국에는 종단이 몇 개나 되나요?

K: 공식적으로 등록된 게 30개가 넘지만 그중 5개 종단이 크지요.

F: 그렇다면 불자는 얼마나 되는데요.

K: 인구의 약 반이 종교인이라면 그중 반 이상이 불자라고 말할 수 있어요.

F: 조계종단의 특징을 말한다면?

K: 글쎄요, 대략적으로밖에 말할 수 없을 것 같아요. 승려의 독신주의, 채식주의, 일 년에 여름 겨울 3개월씩 안거 지키기 등을 들 수 있지만, 무엇보다도 교와 선의 통불교적인 면이 강점이라 말할 수 있지요.

F: 한국의 교회는 어떤가요? 요즘 서구에서는 교회가 사양길이거든요.

K: 한국에서는 그렇지 않아요. 아시다시피, 한국전쟁으로 남북이 분단되었잖아요. 이런 불안한 사회 상황 아래서 전능하신 구세주 이론이 헐벗고 상처받은 사람들한테 잘 먹혀들었고, 경제가 성장하면서 외국, 주로 미국에서 공부하고 돌아온 사람들이 공무원이나 정치가가 되어 정책이 교회에 편향되면서 특히나 개신교들이 엄청 성장하게 되었지요.

Four Great Messages in the Jogye Order (조계종의 4대 종지)

1) No dependence on words and letters (교외별전)
2) Transmission from mind to mind (이심전심)
3) Direct pointing to the heart of man (직지인심)
4) Seeing own nature and attaining Buddhahood (견성성불)

Appendix (부록)

Major Chants 예불문 禮佛文

The Three Refuges 삼귀의 三歸依 (Sam kwi ui)

거룩한 부처님께 귀의합니다. 歸依佛 兩足尊

  (I take refuge in the Buddha.)

거룩한 가르침에 귀의합니다. 歸依法 離欲尊

  (I take refuge in the Dharma)

거룩한 스님들께 귀의합니다. 歸依僧 衆中尊

  (I take refuge in the Sangha)

Yebul (Pay Homage to the Buddha) 예불 禮佛

계향 戒香 Gye hyang

  (May the sweet scent of our keeping the precepts,

정향 定香 Jong hyang

  of our meditations,

혜향 慧香 Hae hyang

  of our wisdom,

해탈향 解脫香 Hae tal hyang

  of our liberation and

해탈지견향 解脫知見香 Hae tal ji gyon hyang

  of the knowledge of our liberation.)

광명운대 주변법계 光明雲臺 周遍法界

Kwang myong un dae ju byon bop kae

  (May all this form a shining cloud-like pavilion and pervade the
  whole universe.)

공양시방 무량불법승 供養十方 無量佛法僧

Gong yang shi bang Moo ryang bool bup seung

  (May it do homage to all the countless Buddhas, Dharma and
  Sanghas in all the ten directions.)

헌향진언 獻香眞言 (Mantra of Incense Offering)

옴 바아라 도비야 훔 (3번)

Om ba a ra do bi ya hoom (repeated 3 times)

지심귀명례 삼계도사 사생자부 시아본사 석가모니불

至心歸命禮 三界導師 四生慈父 是我本師 釋迦牟尼佛

Ji shim kwi myong nae Sam gye do sa Sa saeng ja bu Shi a bon sa
So ga mo ni bul

  (We most devoutly pay homage to the teacher of all the three
  worlds, the great teacher of all beings, to our guide, Sakyamuni
  Buddha.)

지심귀명례 시방삼세 제망찰해 상주일체 불타야중

至心歸命禮 十方三世 帝網刹海 常住一切 佛陀耶衆

Ji shim kwi myong nae Shi bang sam sae Jae mang chal hae Sang ju il chae Bul ta ya joong

(We most devoutly pay homage to the eternally existent assembly of all the Buddhas, in all the ten directions, throughout the past, present and future, as countless as the lands and seas in Lord Indras net.)

지심귀명례 시방삼세 제망찰해 상주일체 달마야중

至心歸命禮 十方三世 帝網刹海 常住一切 達摩耶衆

Ji shim kwi myong nae Shi bang sam sae jae mang chal hae Sang ju il chae dal ma ya joong

(We most devoutly pay homage to all the eternally existent Teachings, in all the ten directions, throughout the past, present and future as countless as the lands and seas in Lord Indras' net)

지심귀명례 대지문수 사리보살 대행보현보살 대비관세음보살 대원 본존 지장보살마하살

至心歸命禮 大智文殊 舍利菩薩 大行普賢菩薩 大悲觀世音菩薩 大願 本尊 地藏菩薩摩訶薩

Ji shim kwi myong nae Dae ji mun su sa li bosal dae haeng bo hyun bo sal Dae bee kwan se um bo sal Dae won bon jon ji jang bo sal Ma ha sal

(We most devoutly pay homage to all Bodhisattvas and Mahasattvas, and especially do we commemorate the Bodhisattvas Manjusri, Sariputra, Samantabhadra, the most compassionate and loving Avalokiteshvara, and he, the Lord of many vows, Ksitigarbha.)

지심귀명례 영산당시 수불부촉 십대제자 십육성 오백성 독수성 내지 천이백 제대아라한 무량자비성중 至心歸命禮 靈山當時 受佛附囑 十大弟子 十六聖 五百聖 獨修聖 乃至 千二百 諸大阿羅漢 無量慈悲聖衆

Ji shim kwi myong nae Young san dang shi su bul bu chok ship dae jae ja Ship yuk song o baek sung dok su sung nae ji Chun e baek jae dae arahan mu ryang ja bi song joong

(We most devoutly pay homage to the countless compassionate and love-filled communities, and most especially do we commemorate those who have received personally the Buddhas teachings on Mount Gridhakuta; the ten major disciples, the sixteen arhats, the five-hundred saints, the saints who practiced alone, and all of the one thousand two hundred great arhats.)

지심귀명례 서건동진 급아해동 역대전등 제대조사 천하종사 일체미진수 제대선지식 至心歸明禮 西乾東震 及我海東 歷代 傳燈 諸大祖師 天下宗師 一切微塵數 諸大善知識

Ji shim kwi myong nae Suh gun dong jin Geub ah hae dong Yok dae jeon dung Je dae jo sa Chun ha jong sa Il che mee jin soo Je dae son jee shik

(We most devoutly pay homage to those great patriarchs and teachers who have come from the West to the East, those who have come to Korean shores, and who have transmitted the Light of the Teaching down through all generations. Likewise we pay homage to masters of all traditions, recognized throughout the ages and to our various numberless spiritual teachers and friends.)

지심귀명례 시방삼세 제망찰해 상주일체 승가야중

至心歸命禮 十方三世 帝網刹海 常住一切 僧伽耶衆

Ji shim kwi myong nae Shi bang sam sae je mang chal hae Sang ju il chae seung ga ya joong

(We most devoutly pay homage tothe eternally existent of all Sanghas, in all the ten directions, throughout the past, present, and future as countless as the lands and seas in Lord Indras net.)

유원 무진삼보 대자대비 수아정례 명훈가피력 원공법계 제중생 자 타일시 성불도 唯願 無盡三寶 大慈大悲 受我頂禮 冥熏加被力 願共 法界諸衆生 自他一時 成佛道

Yu won mu jin sam bo Dae ja dae bee Su a jong nae Myong hoon ga pi ruk Won gong bub gye Je jung saeng Ja ta il shi Sung bul doh

(We most earnestly desire that these inexhaustible Three Jewels will most lovingly and compassionately receive our devotions, and that they will empower us spiritually; furthermore, we vow that, together with all sentient beings throughout the dharma realms, we may all attain Buddhahood at one and the same time.)

마하반야바라밀다심경 摩訶般若波羅蜜多心經

Ma ha ban ya ba ra mil da shim kyong

(Homage to the Perfection of Wisdom, the Lovely, the Holy!)

관자재보살 觀自在菩薩

kwan ja jae bosal

행심반야바라밀다시 行深般若波羅密多時

haeng shim ban ya ba ra mil da shi

조견오온개공도일체고액 照見五蘊皆空 度一切苦厄

Jo gyon o on gae gong do il che go aek

(Avalokiteshvara Bodhisattva was practicing the profound wisdom which has gone beyond and gazed down from on high and saw that all five components are empty, and was freed form all suffering and distress.)

사리자 舍利子 sa ri ja

색불이공 공불이색 色不異空 空不異色

Saek bul e gong gong bul e saek

색즉시공 공즉시색 色卽是空 空卽是色

Saek juk shi gong gong juk shi saek

수상행식 역부여시 受想行識 亦復如是

Su sang heng shik yok bu yo shi

(O Sariputra, form is emptiness, emptiness is form; form does not differ from emptiness, emptiness does not differ form; whatever is empty, that is form, whatever is form that is empty. The same is true of feelings, perceptions, impulses and consciousness.)

사리자 舍利子 시제법공상 是諸法空相

Sa ri ja shi jeh bub gong sang

불생불멸 불구부정 부증불감 不生不滅 不垢不淨 不增不減

Bul saeng bul myol Bul gu bu jong Bu jeung bul gahm

(O Sariputra, all dharmas are marked by emptiness, they have no beginning and no end, they are neither impure nor pure, they neither increase nor decrease.)

시고 공중무색 무수상행식 是故 空中無色 無受想行識

shi go gong joong mu saek mu su sang haeng shik

(Therefore, in emptiness there is no form, no feeling, no perception, no impulses, no consciousness.)

무안이비설신의 무색성향미촉법 無眼耳鼻舌身意 無色聲香味觸法

Mu an e bi sol shin e mu saek sung hyang mi chok bop

(No eye, no ear, no nose, no tongue, no body, no mind; no forms, sounds, smells, tastes, touches, objects of the mind.)

무안계 내지 무의식계 無眼界 乃至 無意識界

Mu an gae nae ji mu ui shik gae

(No visual sphere up to no consciousness sphere)

무무명 역무무명진 無無明 亦無無明盡

Mu mu myong Yok mu mu myong jin

내지 무노사 역무노사진 乃至 無老死 亦無老死盡

nae ji Mu no sa yok mu no sa jin

(No ignorance and or extinction of it, upto no old age and death, and no extinction of old age and death.)

무고집멸도 무지역무득 이무소득고 無苦集滅道 無智亦無得 以無所得故

Mu go jib myol do mu ji yok mu duk E mu so duk go

(There is no suffering, no origination, no cessation or no path; no cognition, and also no attainment, for there is nothing to attain.)

보리살타 의반야바라밀다고 菩提薩埵 依般若波羅密多故

bo li sal ta ui ban ya ba la mil ta go

심무가애 무가애고 心無罣碍 無罣碍故

Shim mu ga ae mu ga ae go

무유공포 원리전도몽상 無有恐怖 遠離顛倒夢想

Mu yu gong po wol li jon do mong sang

구경열반 삼세제불 의반야바라밀다 究竟涅槃 三世諸佛 依般若波羅蜜多

Gu gyong yol ban Sam sae jae bul Ui ban ya ba la mil ta

고득 아뇩다라삼먁삼보리 故得 阿耨多羅三藐三菩提

Go duk anyok dara sam myak sam bo li

(Bodhisattvas rely on the Perfection of Wisdom and are mentally unburdened. With no mental obstacles, they have no fears or fantasies, and they attain the ultimate Nirvana, All Buddhas who appear in the three periods rely on the perfection of wisdom, and awake to the utmost, right and perfect enlightenment.)

고지반야바라밀다 故知 般若波羅蜜多

Go ji ban ya bra la mil ta

시대신주 시대명주 是大神呪 是大明呪

Shi dae shin ju shi dae myong ju

시무상주 시무등등주 능제일체고 是無上呪 是無等等呪 能除一切苦

Shi mu sang ju shi mu dung dung ju Neung je il che go

  (Therefore, one should know the perfection of wisdom is the great mantra, the unsurpassed mantra, the unequaled mantra, the destroyer of all suffering.)

진실불허 고설 眞實不虛 故說

jin shil bul huh go sol

반야바라밀다주 즉설주왈 般若波羅蜜多呪 卽說 呪曰

Ban ya ba ra mil ta ju juk sol ju wal

  (This is true and not false. So recite the perfection of Wisdom mantra; recite the mantra that says:)

아제아제 바라아제 바라승아제 모지 사바하

揭諦揭諦 婆羅揭諦 婆羅僧揭諦 菩堤 娑婆訶 (3번)

A jae a jae ba ra a jae ba ra sung a jae mo ji sabaha (repeated 3 times)

Gate, gate, paragate, parasamgate, bodhi, svaha!

Gate, gate, paragate, parasamgate, bodhi, svaha!

Gate, gate, paragate, parasamgate, bodhi, svaha!

  (Gone, gone, gone beyond, gone utterly beyond, enlightenment, hail!)

나의 한글 반야심경

성스러운 관세음보살이 심오한 지혜의 완성을 실천하실 때 (관자재보살 행심 반야바라밀다 시) 존재하는 것은 다섯 가지의 요소(오온)로 구성되어 있다는 것을 아셨다.

그러나 이 구성요소는 그 본질에서 실체가 없다는 것을 비추어 보시고 일체의 괴로움을 제도해 주셨다. (조견오온 개공도 일체고액)

사리자여, 이 세상의 물질적 현상은 실체가 없다. (사리자, 색불이공) 그러나 실체는 없지만 물질 현상을 떠나 있는 것은 아니다. (공불이색) 물질적 현상이라는 것은 모두 실체가 없고 (색즉시공) 실체가 없다는 것은 물질 현상인 것이다. (공즉시색)

느낌과 생각, 의지와 의식 작용도 모두 실체가 없다. (수상행식 역부여시)

사리자여, 이 세상 모든 존재는 실체가 없다는 특성이 있어 (제법공상) 생기고 없어지는 것이 없으며 (불생불멸) 더럽거나 깨끗한 것이 없으며 (불구부정) 늘어남도 줄어듦도 없다. (부증불감)

그러기에 사리자여, 실체가 없다는 입장에서는 물질적 현상, 느낌, 생각, 의지, 의식도 없다. (공중무색 무수상행식)

눈, 귀, 코, 혀, 몸, 뜻의 감각주체가 없고 (무안이비설신의) 그 경계인 모양, 소리, 냄새, 맛, 감촉, 마음의 대상이 없다. (무색성향미촉법)

눈의 영역에서 의식의 영역에 이르기까지 모든 것이 없다. (무안계 내지무의식계)

무명이 없고 무명이 다함이 없다. (무무명 역무무명진)

게다가 늙고 죽음도 없으며, (내지 무노사) 끝내 늙고 죽음을 벗어나는 길도 없나니 (역무노사진) 괴로움도 없고 괴로움의 원인도 없고 괴로움을 벗어날 길도 없느니라. (무고집멸도)

지혜가 따로 있을 수 없으며 (무지역무득) 얻음과 잃을 것이 없으므로 (이무소득고) 모든 보살은 반야바라밀다에 의지하여 닦아가나니 (보리살타 의반야바라밀다고) 마음에 걸림이 없고 걸림이 없기에 (무가애고) 두려움이 없어 (무유공포) 뒤바뀐 헛된 망상을 떠나 (원리전도몽상) 마침내 열반에 이르느니라. (구경열반)

과거, 현재, 미래의 모든 부처님들이 (삼세제불) 반야바라밀다를 의지하여 (의반야바라밀다) 무상정등정각을 얻었으니 (고득 아눗다라삼먁삼보리) 이 반야바라밀다는 가장 신비하고, (시대신주) 크고 밝은 진언이며 (시대명주) 위없는 진언이며 (시무상주) 견줄 데 없는 진언이니 (시무등등주) 능히 온갖 괴로움을 없애고 (능제일체고) 참으로 진실하여 허망하지 않느니라. (진실불허)

이제 반야바라밀다의 주문을 말하노라. (고설 반야바라밀다주 즉설주왈)

아제 아제 바라 아제 바라 승아제 모지 사바하

(가는 자여, 가는 자여, 피안으로 가는 자여, 피안으로 온전히 가는 자여, 깨달음 얻으리.)

(반야심경을 독송하면서 '심경의 심오한 뜻을 조금이라도 쉽게 풀어 독송할 수 없을까' 하는 생각이 항상 머리를 떠나지 않았다. 여러 버전을 살펴보다가. 초심자 시절에 시어머님께서 주신 『일상생활불교 성전』(보련각 1979)이 생각났다. 그때는 애들이 어려서 절에 갈 여유가 없었다. 당연 이 판본도 전부 이해되지 않았으나 한자말보다는 훨씬 쉬웠다.

'색이 곧 공이요 공이 곧 색이니, 수상행식도 그러하니라'는 우리말인데

도 무슨 뜻인지 전혀 짐작할 수 없는 표준판본보다 우선 친절했고 짐작
이 되었다.

종단에서 얼마나 많은 토론과 숙의를 거쳐 표준판본을 만들었을까 모
르는 바 아니다. 부처님 가르침은 명확한데 언제까지 알 듯 모를 듯한
말로 독송해야 하나 하는 안타까움에서 여러 본을 저본 삼아 감히 내
나름으로 편집하여 실어본다. 나무 마하반야바라밀)

Four Great Vows 사홍서원 四弘誓願 (Sah hong so won)

중생무변 서원도 衆生無邊誓願度

Jung seng mu byun so won doh (I vow to save all beings)

번뇌무진 서원단 煩惱無盡誓願斷

Byon nae mu jin so won dan (I vow to end all sufferings)

법문무량 서원학 法門無量誓願學

Bop mun mu yang so won hak (I vow to learn all Dharma
teachings)

불도무상 서원성 佛道無上誓願成

Bul do mu sang so won sung (I vow to attain Enlightenment)

법성게: 해인 법계도

(Uisang's Ocean Seal of Hwaom Buddhism)

1. 법성원융무이상 法性圓融無二相

   Since dharma-nature is complete and interpenetrating.

   It is without any sign of duality.

2. 제법부동본래적 諸法不動本來寂

   All dharmas are unmoving and originally calm.

3. 무명무상절일체 無名無相絶一切

   With no name, no form, all (distinctions) are abolished.

4. 증지소지비여경 證智所知非餘境

   It is known through the wisdom of enlightenment, not by any
   other level.

5. 진성심심극미묘 眞性甚深極微妙

   The true-nature is extremely profound, exceedingly subtle and
   sublime.

6. 불수자성수연성 不守自性隨緣成

   It does not attach to self-nature, but manifests following
   (causal) conditions.

7. 일중일체다중일 一中一切多中一

   In one is all and in many is one.

8. 일즉일체다즉일 一卽一切多卽一

   One is identical to all, and many is identical to One.

9. 일미진중함시방 一微塵中含十方

In one particle of dust is contained the ten directions.

10. 일체진중역여시 一切塵中亦如是

And so it is with all particles of dust.

11. 무량원겁즉일념 無量遠劫卽一念

Incalculably long eons are identical to a single thought-instant.

12. 일념즉시무량겁 一念卽是無量劫

And a single thought-instant is identical to incalculably long eons.

13. 구세십세호상즉 九世十世互相卽

The nine times and the ten times are mutually identical.

14. 잉불잡란격별성 仍不雜亂隔別成

Yet are not confused or mixed but function separately.

15. 초발심시변정각 初發心時便正覺

The moment one begins to aspire with their heart, instantly perfect enlightenment (is attained.)

16. 생사열반상공화 生死涅槃相共和

Samsara and Nirvana are always harmonized together.

17. 이사명연무분별 理事冥然無分別

Particular-phenomena and Universal-principle are completely merged without distinction.

18. 십불보현대인경 十佛普賢大人境

This is the world of the Bodhisattva Samantabhadra, and this is the world of greatness.

19. 능인해인삼매중 能仁海印三昧中

   In the Ocean-Seal-Samadhi of the Buddha.

20. 번출여의부사의 繁出如意不思議

   Many unimaginable (miracles) are produced according to one's wishes.

21. 우보익생만허공 雨寶益生滿虛空

   This shower of jewels benefitting all sentient beings, fills the whole of empty space.

22. 중생수기득이익 衆生隨器得利益

   All sentient beings receive this wealth according to their capacities.

23. 시고행자환본제 是故行者還本際

   Therefore, he who practices contemplation returns to the primordial realm.

24. 파식망상필부득 叵息妄想必不得

   And without cutting off ignorance, it cannot be obtained.

25. 무연선교착여의 無緣善巧捉如意

   By unconditional expedient means, one attains complete freedom.

26. 귀가수분득자량 歸家隨分得資糧

   Returning home (the primordial realm) you obtain riches according to your capacity.

27. 이다라니무진보 以陀羅尼無盡寶

By means of this Dharani, an inexhaustible treasure,

28. 장엄법계실보전 莊嚴法界實寶殿

One adorns the dharmadhatu, as a real palace of jewels.

29. 궁좌실제중도상 窮坐實際中道床

Finally, one reposes in the real world, the bed of the Middle Way.

30. 구래부동명위불 舊來不動名爲佛

That which is originally without motion, named Buddha.

혜국스님 법성게 해설

1. 법성원융무이상

우주의 진리 법의 성품에는 잘났다 못났다, 나다 너다 하는 차별상이 본래 없으니 "법성은 원융하여 두 모양이 본래 없고"

2. 제법부동본래적

삼라만상의 근본인 법의 본질에는 존재 원리가 모두 평등하여 영원한 대자유라 "모든 법이 고요하여 움직임이 본래 없다"

3. 무명무상절일체

이러한 모든 생명의 여여한 본질은 어떠한 언어로도 표현할 수 없는 까닭에 "일체가 끊어져서 이름도 없고, 모양도 없으니"

4. 증지소지비여경

존재의 원리인 중도를 깨달은 지혜로 볼 뿐, 생각으로 알 수가 없는 연고로 "깨친 지혜로 알 뿐 다른 경계로 알 수 없네"

5. 진성심심극미묘

   법성의 참성품은 그윽하고 미묘하여 생각으로 도저히 미칠 수
   없는 미묘한 자리라 "진성은 깊고 깊어 지극히 미묘하며"

6. 불수자성수연성

   고정된 자기 성품이 없어 나라는 고집이 없으니 오직 인연따라
   나타날 뿐이라 "자성이 따로 없어 인연따라 나타나네"

7. 일중일체다중일

   지구별 하나 안에 온갖 삼라만상이 다모여도 모자람 없으니
   법의 공성에는 "하나 안에 일체가 있고 일체 안에 하나 있어"

8. 일즉일체다즉일

   하나와 전체는 크다, 작다를 비교할 때만 생겨날 뿐, 텅빈
   공에서는 없는 일이라 "하나가 곧 전체요, 전체가 하나니라"

9. 일미진중함시방

   한 송이 꽃 속에 우주 기운 들어있고 떨어지는 낙엽에도
   가을이 들었으니 "한 티끌 안에 온 우주를 머금었고"

10. 일체진중역여시

조그만 티끌 하나하나에도 본질 찾아 들어가면 그 근본은 모두가
공이러니 "모든 티끌 하나마다 온 법계가 들어있다"

11.무량원겁즉일념

무량한 긴 시간도 근본을 바로 보면 바닷물에 파도 일 듯이
한 생각 일어남이니 "시작 없는 무량겁이 한 생각 찰나요"

12. 일념즉시무량겁

한 생각 일어남이 곧 무량한 시간이라 법성에서는 찰나와 무량겁
이 같은 말이니 "찰나의 한 생각 그대로 무량겁이라"

13. 구세십세호상즉

시간과 공간을 초월하니 구세라는 현상계나 십세라는 법계진리
애당초 둘 아니니 "현상과 진리가 하나되어 춤을 추네"

14. 잉불잡란격별성

천만 개의 등불을 키더라도 서로 장애되는 일 없이 오직 제
밝음만 지켜가니 "혼란 없이 분명하여 따로따로 나투었네"

15. 초발심시변정각

법성의 존재원리가 처음 내는 마음이나 깨친 마음이나 한결같은
마음이니 "처음 발심 그 마음이 정각을 이룬 때라"

16. 생사열반상공화

나고 죽음이 서로 다른 이름일 뿐 생사니 열반이니 둘이 아닌
본래 한 자리 "생사와 열반 경계 그 근본이 한 몸이네"

17. 이사명연무분별

근본 진리와 현상 경계가 텅 빈 공성이라 분별할 수 없거니와
본시 확연하니 "이사가 분명하여 분별할 길 본래 없으니"

18. 십불보현대인경

모든 부처님과 모든 보살과 법성을 깨달은 이들 다같이
성인들의 경계이니 "재불 보살이 모두가 성인들의 경계로다"

19. 능인해인삼매중

일체의 번뇌망상이 끊어진 자리, 한 생각 나기 이전 무념처라
공적영지이니 "부처님의 거룩한 법, 번뇌 없는 해인 삼매"

20. 번출여의부사의

의심이나 생각으로 헤아릴 수 없는 세계라 마음따라 자재하게
드러나나니 "부사의 무궁한 법 임의자재 드러나네"

21. 우보익생만허공

삼천세계 두루한 것이 법성의 원리. 모든 중생들에게 이로운 비
온누리에 가득하니 "일체중생 유익하게 온법계에 감로비라"

22. 중생수기득이익

중생들의 역량따라 근기가 달라 그릇만큼 유익함을 저마다
얻게 되니 "중생 근기, 그릇따라 온갖 이익 얻게하네"

23. 시고행자환본제

번뇌 망상 모두 쉬고 마음 깨친 수행자는 본래 부처 그 자리에
곧바로 돌아가니 "그러므로 수행자는 근본으로 돌아가서"

24. 파식망상필부득

번뇌 망상 없애려고 많은 세월 보냈건만 망상이 보리이니
그 진리를 바로 보면 "망상을 쉬려해도 그 망상이 따로 없네"

25.무연선교착여의

깨달음에는 기교나 방편 본래 없나니 기특한 길 따로 없어
그대로 여여하니 "무연자비 거룩한 법 마음 따라 자재하니"

26. 귀가수분득자량

스스로 존재하는 존재원리라 이름하여 그 마음 성취하고
본고향 돌아오니 "보리 열반 성취하여 본래 마음 깨달았네"

27. 이다라니무진보

차별 없는 법성의 진리 청정하고 다함없는 법성게 법문

무량한 보배이니 "이 다라니 무진 법문 한량 없는 보배로다"

28. 장엄법계실보전

한 마음이 청정하니 청정장엄이라 곳곳마다 불국토요

장엄정토를 나투시니 "청정법계 장엄하여 불국토를 나투시고"

29. 궁좌실제중도상

공에서 깨고 나니 본시 그 사람 법의 성품 여여하고

진여성품 깨고 보니 "본래부터 주인이라 중도임을 깨달으니"

30. 구래부동명위불

그렇게나 육도를 윤회하더니 오고감이 본래 없는 근본자리가

나의 참모습이라 "본래부터 부동하여 그 이름 부처라네"

(충주 석종사 화엄공원에는 법성게가 동강 조수호 선생님의 수려한 글씨의 석비로 조성되어 공원을 장엄하고 있습니다. 그 옆 알림판에는 혜국 큰스님께서 해설하신 법성게 해설문도 나란히 있습니다. 그것을 카메라에 담아 와서 불자님들의 이해를 돕기 위하여 여기 옮겨봅니다.)

참고한 책들

- *The Awakening of Faith* translated with commentary by Yoshito S. Hakoda (Columbia University Press)
- *The Zen Monastic Experience* by Robert E Buswell Jr. (Princeton University Press)
- *Opening the Heart of the Cosmos* by Thich Nhat Hanh (Parallax Press, Berkeley, CA)
- *Nine Mountains: Dharma-Lectures of the Korean Meditation Master Kusan* (International Meditation Center Song Kwangsa Monastery)
- *What is Korean Buddhism* (Jogye Order Publishing 2007)
- *Understanding Korean Buddhism* (Jogye Order Publishing 2007)
- *The Most Joyful Study: The Dharma Talks of Cheongwha Sunim* (Muju Publishing Inc. 2008)
- *Korean Temple Motifs: Beautiful Symbols of the Buddhist Faith* by Heo Gyun (Dolbagae Publishers)
- *Historical Dictionary of Buddhism* by Charles S. Prebish (Sri Sataru Publications)
- *Everyday Korean Buddhist practices* by Zen Master Ilta, Translated by Brian Barry

고연희(묘심월)

이화여대 영문과를 졸업하고 동국대 부설 사회교육원(현 미래융합교
육원)의 불교영어/불교전문반에서 수학하였다.
대한불교조계종 국제포교사 품수를 받고 국제포교사회 부회장을
역임하였다. 조계사 외국인 안내소에서 사찰안내, 불교문화사업
단에서 외국인을 위한 템플스테이 안내 및 통역 등의 자원봉사 활
동을 하였다.

궁금하세요? 우리 절집
HANDBOOK FOR EXPLORING KOREAN TEMPLES

초판 1쇄 발행 2021년 11월 12일 | 초판 2쇄 발행 2023년 7월 28일
엮은이 고연희 | 펴낸이 김시열
펴낸곳 도서출판 운주사

(02832) 서울시 성북구 동소문로 67-1 성심빌딩 3층
전화 (02) 926-8361 | 팩스 0505-115-8361
ISBN 978-89-5746-662-9 03220 값 14,800원
http://cafe.daum.net/unjubooks 〈다음카페: 도서출판 운주사〉